A Short History of Cheap Music

As Exemplified in the Records of the House of Novello, Ewer & Co., with Special Reference to the First Fifty Years of the Reign of Her Most Gracious Majesty, Queen Victoria

GEORGE GROVE

CAMBRIDGE UNIVERSITY PRESS

Cambridge New York Melbourne Madrid Cape Town Singapore São Paolo Delhi

Published in the United States of America by Cambridge University Press, New York

www.cambridge.org
Information on this title: www.cambridge.org/9781108001700

© in this compilation Cambridge University Press 2009

This edition first published 1887
This digitally printed version 2009

ISBN 978-1-108-00170-0

This book reproduces the text of the original edition. The content and language reflect
the beliefs, practices and terminology of their time, and have not been updated.

CAMBRIDGE LIBRARY COLLECTION
Books of enduring scholarly value

Music
The systematic academic study of music gave rise to works of description, analysis and criticism, by composers and performers, philosophers and anthropologists, historians and teachers, and by a new kind of scholar - the musicologist. This series makes available a range of significant works encompassing all aspects of the developing discipline.

A Short History of Cheap Music
The publisher Novello was hugely influential in making music affordable for a wider section of the Victorian public. A Short History of Cheap Music, published in 1887, focuses on Novello's role and draws on the company's archives. It begins with the establishment of the house in 1811, when the founder, Vincent Novello, printed his first book at his own personal expense. Soon afterwards the house made available cheap editions of major musical compositions including Mozart's and Haydn's Masses, Purcell's sacred music, and various Italian and English works. It also printed a variety of publications and journals dedicated to music, advocated the reduction of taxes on music, and organised events for the advancement of the musical arts. The author shows how by finding cheaper methods for printing music, organising cheap concerts, and establishing new choral societies, the house of Novello gradually created a taste for music among new audiences, a process paralleled today in the new media.

Cambridge University Press has long been a pioneer in the reissuing of out-of-print titles from its own backlist, producing digital reprints of books that are still sought after by scholars and students but could not be reprinted economically using traditional technology. The Cambridge Library Collection extends this activity to a wider range of books which are still of importance to researchers and professionals, either for the source material they contain, or as landmarks in the history of their academic discipline.

Drawing from the world-renowned collections in the Cambridge University Library, and guided by the advice of experts in each subject area, Cambridge University Press is using state-of-the-art scanning machines in its own Printing House to capture the content of each book selected for inclusion. The files are processed to give a consistently clear, crisp image, and the books finished to the high quality standard for which the Press is recognised around the world. The latest print-on-demand technology ensures that the books will remain available indefinitely, and that orders for single or multiple copies can quickly be supplied.

The Cambridge Library Collection will bring back to life books of enduring scholarly value across a wide range of disciplines in the humanities and social sciences and in science and technology.

A SHORT HISTORY

OF

CHEAP MUSIC.

VINCENT NOVELLO.

A SHORT HISTORY

OF

CHEAP MUSIC

AS EXEMPLIFIED IN THE RECORDS OF THE HOUSE

OF

NOVELLO, EWER & CO.

WITH ESPECIAL REFERENCE TO THE FIRST FIFTY YEARS

OF THE REIGN OF

HER MOST GRACIOUS MAJESTY

QUEEN VICTORIA

WITH THREE PORTRAITS

AND A PREFACE BY SIR GEORGE GROVE, D.C.L., &c

LONDON & NEW YORK
NOVELLO, EWER AND CO.
1887.

PREFACE.

THE following record of the rise and progress of an eminent London publishing-house forms a chapter of extreme interest in the history of the century, and more especially of the reign of Queen Victoria. It furnishes a typical instance of the combination of intelligence, foresight, and energy, which distinguishes that period. It exemplifies the rise, we might almost say the creation, of a new intellectual class of the people, and the prodigious progress that has been made in supplying that class, not with exciting and deleterious means of subsistence, but with the food best adapted for its solid growth. It chronicles an advance of which we may be proud in one of the highest departments of mental progress and one of the noblest of the arts—an advance which may claim a special merit among the great movements of the day, because music ministers to the imagination of man, and leaves untouched his baser faculties. This may be emphatically said of the noble music which forms the foundation of the fabric raised by the house of Novello.

Moreover, this record shows how dependent men and things are on one another, and how secure those undertakings are which rise from small beginnings. Vincent Novello might have been as musical as he was, Alfred Novello as far-sighted, and Henry Littleton as enterprising and as accurate; but it would all have been to no purpose but for the progress made in machinery and practical science, for the increase in communication, and for the removal of the taxes on literature, which have distinguished the reign of our beloved Sovereign; that removal being itself greatly aided by one of the three enlightened and energetic men just mentioned. The same causes which have created the immense periodical literature of our day have brought about the equally extraordinary cheap music which we now possess, and while they have given us the *Daily Telegraph* for a penny and the *Illustrated London News* for sixpence, have also given us a still more valuable acquisition—*The Messiah* and *Israel in Egypt* for a shilling. It is the division of labour, the spread of machinery, the extension of travelling and transport, the invention and use of labour-saving processes of all kinds unknown to former generations, and also the progress of education, helped by the foregoing mechanical improvements, and itself re-acting strongly on them—it is these characteristic achievements of the reign of Victoria which have effected so much in literature and music that is a mere commonplace to us, but which to our fathers and grandfathers was unknown, unexpected, impossible, and, we may add, not desired, because the desire had not been evoked. When the house of Novello was founded no one could have dreamed of the change that was so soon to arrive. When the present writer was in his teens, the price of music was more than twenty times what it now is. The first guinea that he recollects having had given to him, in 1837, was expended in a pianoforte score of *The Messiah* which is now published at a shilling. Good music at all out of the common line was either enormously dear or in manuscript, and had to be copied at the British Museum. The publications of the house of Novello and its imitators have altered all this, and have banished to the shelf a mass of copies of old Italian and old English music made during hundreds of delightful half-hours snatched from the day's work in the old reading room in Montague Place, long before the building of Panizzi's dome. Not that this labour was useless. On the contrary, it was fraught with good. The searching for the works, the balancing of one service, motett, madrigal, or cantata against another, the eager poring over the many volumes of Burney's Extracts, Tudway, or Needler's Collection, forced one involuntarily into the acquisition of much knowledge. Further, this copying taught one clefs and figured bass; it obliged one to play from score or to write one's own accompaniment—in fact, gave one knowledge against one's will for which the modern student has little or no occasion.

But enough of this *laudatio temporis acti*. Suffice it to say that things were so; and so they would have continued, and all improvements in material matters would have been useless, but for the enterprise and sharp-sightedness which enabled our Novellos and Littletons to foresee where and how the public could be attacked, where an improvement could be introduced or an amelioration suggested, where a want could be discovered or made to create itself, which the new resources could supply.

We have spoken above of small beginnings; and surely a better or more instructive example can hardly be found than is given by the history of this firm. The migrations from the private house of the venerable Founder to Frith Street, from that to Dean Street, and from that again to the vast edifice in Berners Street, with its handmaid establishments in London and New York, mark the sure and certain advance due to sound caution.

All this will be found, as far as the house of Novello & Co. and its connections are concerned, in the following pages, and a most interesting and instructive record it presents. If it had only revived our recollection of Vincent Novello, to whom we are apt to forget our deep debt of gratitude, it would have done much; but the whole narrative is full of wider interest, and forms a very important addition to the history of the country. The real symbols of the firm are Vincent's two successors, and it is seldom that we are supplied with the details of such ceaseless activity in such a sphere, or have the opportunity of penetrating into the secret recesses of a house of business, of coming face to face with the actual individuals who have seen so clearly and achieved so much, or of tracing the onward steps of their honourable progress towards an enormous business and the wealth which is its inevitable accompaniment. The mere catalogue of the valuable works brought out, the ceaseless spread of the action of the firm, the way in which Germany, Italy, France, America, are one by one annexed by these peaceful conquerors—not only keeps one in continual astonishment, but excites one's gratitude for a record at once so interesting, so important for the historian, and so eminently characteristic of the great Nineteenth Century.

GEORGE GROVE.

June 14, 1887.

CONTENTS.

	PAGE
INTRODUCTION. 1811—1836	1
CHAPTER I. 1837—1847	17
CHAPTER II. 1848—1857	45
CHAPTER III. 1858—1867	73
CHAPTER IV. 1868—1877	101
CHAPTER V. 1878—1887	123
INDEX	143

PORTRAITS.

VINCENT NOVELLO	Frontispiece
J. ALFRED NOVELLO	To face page 17
HENRY LITTLETON	To face page 73

INTRODUCTION.

1811—1836.

"When there was no music."
Much Ado about Nothing, Act ii., Sc. 3.

THE establishment of the publishing house dates from the year 1811, when Vincent Novello, then in his thirtieth year, issued his "Collection of Sacred Music," in two folio volumes, dedicated to the Rev. Victor Fryer. The expenses of engraving and printing these volumes were provided for by himself out of his hard earnings as a professor of music: no publisher was to be found who would undertake the risk of giving the works to the world, so he himself became perforce his own publisher, and thus laid the foundation of the house. These works, performed by the members of the choir in the chapel of the Portuguese Embassy, in South Street, Park Lane, where he was organist, literally created the taste for compositions of a like kind.

One of the peculiarities of the publication was the addition of an accompaniment for the organ fully set out, and not merely indicated by means of a figured bass. This was an innovation not at all approved by the generality of organists, probably because much of the difficulty and the mystery of their art was smoothed away, and made clear and available for the less skilful. The utility of the plan was silently recognised, and in course of time became general. At this present period no organist would think of printing an accompanying part with a figured bass only, and the school of players who persistently set their faces against the use of other means than the *basso continuo* has few, if any, representatives.

Novello's earliest publications were at first restricted to those required for the Ritual of the Roman Catholic Church, under whose guidance he had been educated. He officiated as deputy for Samuel Webbe the elder, the famous glee writer, at the Sardinian Chapel in Lincoln's Inn Fields, and for John Danby, another glee composer, who was organist of the Chapel of the Spanish Embassy, Manchester Square, and he had thus learned where improvement was possible in the list of works in ordinary use. His arrangement of Reading's Portuguese Hymn, "Adeste Fideles," established its popularity. His second publication, "A Collection of Motetts for the Offertory; and other pieces, principally adapted for the Morning Service," in twelve books, was for many years the standard work of its kind. This was followed, in 1816, by "Twelve easy Masses for Small Choirs," three volumes, and, in 1822, by "The Evening Service, being a collection of pieces appropriate to Vespers, Complin and Tenebrae, including the whole of the Gregorian Hymns for every principal festival throughout the year," in twelve books, or two volumes complete. By the end of 1825 a collection of Mozart's and Haydn's Masses, one in eighteen, the other in sixteen books; a selection from the music in the Fitzwilliam Museum at Cambridge,

Purcell's Sacred Music. 5

five volumes, and other works had been added. None of these works had ever been printed in Vocal Score, and many had never been printed in any form whatever.

In the year 1829 his son, Joseph Alfred [born 1810], commenced business as a publisher at 67, Frith Street, Soho, and his first important work, a continuation of "Purcell's Sacred Music," begun by his father in December, 1828, was completed in seventy-two numbers in October, 1832. The last number was followed by a Life of Purcell, written by Vincent Novello. The work was afterwards (1842-44) issued by Alfred Novello in four volumes, in the same form and exact size of the Musical Antiquarian Society's publications. This was done by arrangement with the society, and many of its subscribers became subscribers to the edition of Purcell.

The issue of this work marks a distinct era in the records of the house and of the history of publishing, and was alone sufficient to prove to the musical world that artistic necessities were even at this early date foreseen and provided for. The majority of the compositions included in this edition had never before appeared in print. It was the first collection of music which Vincent Novello had edited for the Service of a Church outside the pale in which he had been educated. It was also the only important series of collected pieces for the use of the Anglican Church which had been printed since the time of Boyce (Cathedral Music, 1760-78); Arnold (Cathedral Music, 1790); and Page (Harmonia Sacra, 1800).

Previous to these dates, Greene's " Forty Select

Anthems," 1743; Croft's "Thirty Select Anthems," 1724; and Weldon's "Divine Harmony," 1710—all issued by subscription—were the only printed publications available for the use of the choirs of the Anglican Church. All these were in score with figured bass accompaniments. Barnard's "Selected Church Musick, consisting of Services and Anthems, such as are now used in the Cathedral and Collegiate Churches of the Kingdom," printed in 1641, was in separate parts. These separate parts were printed after the manner in which the church books were written at that time and for many years subsequently —namely, with the portions to be sung by the different sides only. Thus the Decani books were useless on the Cantoris side, and the reverse. This process of economising space probably arose at the time when Tallis and Birde enjoyed the monopoly of the patent granted by Queen Elizabeth for printing music and for selling ruled music-paper.* No perfect copy of Barnard's collection is known to exist, and the want of certain of the parts renders the collection almost useless.

It is a somewhat singular fact that when Alfred Novello furnished separate vocal parts for the use of

---

* The patent for the exclusive printing of music-books and selling music-paper was granted to William Birde and Thomas Tallis, on January 22nd, 1575, for twenty-one years, and afterwards continued to Thomas Morley in 1596. One curious result of this monopoly is seen in the character of the written music. To save expense, the notes were written small and close together, so as to get as much as possible on the lines. This, to a certain extent, influenced the character of musical writing, both in manuscript and engraving, even after the patent ceased to be the direct cause of dear ruled paper. The engraved music in " Parthenia," 1611, is an imitation of the written characters employed by Orlando Gibbons, John Bull, and other of the contributors.

choirs, each part complete as far as it went, the older singers strongly objected to the innovation, as it was called. They preferred to sing from the old imperfect manuscript copies or from the printed scores of Boyce, Greene, Croft, Arnold, Page, &c. The neatly engraved oblong editions of the Masses of Haydn and Mozart, which were given to the world at what was then a very cheap rate—the cost of these cheap editions ranging from two shillings to nine and sixpence, each Mass being priced according to size—were looked upon with suspicion, as representing a somewhat dangerous form of revolution in the musical world.

There were but few choral societies in those days, and those that existed were of modest dimensions. One of the most important was the Cecilian Society, which met at the Albion Hall in London Wall, for the practice and performance of Oratorios. The society was wont to advertise as a special attraction that the " Band and Chorus will consist of at least One Hundred Performers," when "The Messiah" was given with Mozart's additional accompaniments. The members of the society were obliged to sing from manuscript copies made by themselves, or, if they possessed them, from the old scores printed by Randall, Harrison, or Arnold ; or from the new editions of certain of Handel's oratorios, edited by Dr. John Clarke, of Cambridge (Clarke-Whitfeld),[*] printed from engraved plates, and

---

[*] He was Professor of Music in the University of Cambridge and Organist of Hereford Cathedral. He adopted the name Whitfeld on the decease of a relative from whom he inherited some property.

published in volumes at two guineas each, by Button and Whitaker, 75, St. Paul's Churchyard, in 1809.

Excepting in the Cathedrals, Anthems and Services were rarely heard. Music, which from the earliest times in the history of the world was courted as the handmaid of devotional exercise, was either grudgingly admitted or totally ignored in the services. There was some curious association between bad singing and religious fervour, the character of the one being increased in proportion to the intensity of the other. The singing of the Charity children was voted a nuisance; no attempt was made to improve the performance of the service in the Parish Churches by careful attention to the science of sweet sounds. The parishioners were content to provide organs, and so long as the player could execute noisy voluntaries, and flood the bad singing with still worse playing, none ever thought of complaining, except a few irritable outsiders who were clamouring for the advance of art in all matters musical.

The attention of the Government had been called to the desirability of teaching music in the National Schools, and the proposal was received with derisive laughter. A few earnest men, like William Edward Hickson, were labouring single-handed in the endeavour to infuse a knowledge of music among the lower classes as a counter-attraction to the charms of the gin-shop. Hickson's labours received an unexpected impetus when Alfred Novello began to publish his cheap music, and the mania for singing classes took hold of the popular mind; these classes received

Cathedral and Church Music. 9

further valuable assistance when John Hullah started his tuneful crusade throughout the length and breadth of the land.*

In the Cathedrals the service was perfunctorily performed, and special complaints, loud and long, were made of the slovenly execution of the music in St. Paul's, London. The old composers were held of small account, until Vincent Novello published his splendid edition of the works of Purcell. This publication gave rise to an annual Purcell Commemoration in Westminster Abbey; and to Novello's earnest endeavours is owing the revival in favour of the works of our native composers.

The Cathedral and musical authorities of the time gave but grudging support to any venture calculated to improve the character of the musical service. They were insensible to the necessity of instituting reforms from within until they felt the pressure from without. This outside pressure was applied in many ways by many bodies working independently and employing moral rather than physical means. The more thoughtful among the musical practitioners hoped, by calling attention to what had been done for the Church by musicians in times past, to awaken attention to matters in the future. Hence the origin of the Musical Antiquarian Society, founded in 1840; and the Motett Society, originated six or seven years later.

Before the death of William the Fourth, Miss

---

* Hullah's " Part Music," compiled for the use of his Upper Singing Classes, was originally published by J. W. Parker, but has since been absorbed into the Catalogue of Novello, Ewer & Co.

Hackett* had made the endeavour to awaken the Cathedral authorities throughout the kingdom to a sense of their duties as concerned the choristers and their education, and the general improvement of Church composition. She offered prizes for the best settings of sacred words for the use of the Church. These were called the Gresham Prize Anthems, and the Cathedral authorities resisted their introduction as long as they could. John Goss's anthem, "Have mercy upon me," one of those to which, in 1833, a prize was awarded, was not sung in the Cathedral of which he was organist until after the year 1860, when a better feeling had arisen, and the disposition to effect reasonable improvements was taking an active form. Old prejudices were fading away, indifference was yielding to active interest, and every endeavour was being made to foster the popular love for music.

During the time that Alfred Novello was in business in Frith Street, many changes and improvements had been introduced and accepted in the art of music printing. Messrs. Clowes had adopted a process of type printing which had been successfully employed for some songs by Henry R. Bishop, and for the *Musical Library*, a publication in which many excellent pieces of music were printed. The value of the process of stereotyping, which had been invented by William Ged, a goldsmith in Edinburgh,

---

* A wealthy amateur, who gave valuable assistance to young musicians belonging to the Cathedrals. At one time Crosby Hall was in her possession, and many concerts were given there through her interest. She died at the age of ninety-one, in 1874, and a tablet to her memory was erected in the crypt of St. Paul's Cathedral by subscriptions from choristers.

so far back as the year 1725, was now recognised.* Printers' workmen no longer mutilated the plates out of hatred for the invention. Experience in use had made the process easy, and although little was added to Ged's system, those who employed it had attained facility in its use, and as it saved the wear of type and the expense of re-composition, it was found to be possible to produce works at a much cheaper rate than heretofore.

In 1834 Alfred Novello moved from Frith Street to 69, Dean Street, the house so long identified with the early operations of the firm, and still used in connection with No. 70 as a printing office. Preston, the music publisher, formerly of 97, Strand, came in his later days to 71, Dean Street, and was succeeded by Coventry and Hollier. So the new house was on a spot already identified with musical enterprise. Soho was fast becoming a musical centre, as in later times Berners Street became. At No. 69 were issued the first numbers of *The Musical World*, a journal which began its career on March 10th, 1836. It appeared weekly for a year and three-quarters, when it changed hands, and was published by H. Hooper for Frederic Davison, of the firm of Gray & Davison, to whom it had been sold by Novello; it afterwards became the property of Messrs. Boosey, and ultimately of J. W. Davison, at whose death it was transferred to the present proprietors.

Like his father, Vincent, who never willingly left a moment unoccupied, Alfred Novello not only gave his

---

* About 1731 Bibles and Prayer Books were stereotyped for the University of Cambridge.

attention to his music business—he was musicseller (by appointment) to Queen Adelaide, consort of William the Fourth—but also earned an excellent reputation as a bass vocalist. He sang at several of the Provincial festivals, and at many of the best of the Metropolitan concerts. He also advertised to "parties interested in the erection of organs in churches, chapels, or music-rooms," offering "material advantage" to them. Under this arrangement, in which his father's judgment was employed, "the grandest instrument in the world—the new organ in the Town Hall, Birmingham"—was built.

Music had not then attained what we now consider to be a cheap stage. "Beethoven's Mass in C, for four voices, with a separate accompaniment for the organ or pianoforte, arranged from the full score, by Vincent Novello," is announced among the lists of new music, "price twelve shillings, separate vocal parts three shillings each." Jacob's National Psalmody, in boards, cost a guinea; a set of Chants for the "Te Deum and Jubilate, and other parts of the Morning and Evening Prayer with the words at length," taken from the above-named work, cost five shillings. Sacred music, so-called, seems to have been restricted to Psalmody as distinct from Anthem music for the majority of the "choirs and places where they sing." The Oratorio of "Judah," selected from Haydn, Mozart, and Beethoven, and called by the name of the compiler as though he were the composer, was to be had, in full score, for three guineas.* The existence

---
* The compiler was William Gardiner, an amateur, of Leicester (born 1770, died 1853). He offered Beethoven a hundred guineas for an overture to this work, but he supposed his letter miscarried, as he never received a reply. He was the

Mendelssohn's "St. Paul." 13

of this thing showed the apathy concerning musical matters at the time. Henry Rowley Bishop's cantata "The Seventh Day," words selected from Milton's "Paradise Lost," was the chief novelty at the time, but it never attained the popularity it deserved. The cheapest copy cost ten shillings.

No cheap copies of Handel's oratorios existed, though every piece in Dr. Clarke's arrangements of Handel's works was printed singly. There was little or no demand, so the supply was limited. Enterprise was not extended to large works, as a general rule. It was therefore with some degree of astonishment, not to say pity, that Mr. Novello's friends in the music trade looked upon him when he purchased the copyright for England of "St. Paul," an oratorio "by Felix Mendelssohn Bartholdi" (*sic*). Yet with this purchase came the dawn of a brighter prospect for the house of Novello, and for the progress of art.

In the advertisement announcing this fact, Mr. Novello says, "The oratorio was first produced at the Düsseldorf festival, on the 22nd May (1836)—of which a detailed account appeared in No. 14 of *The Musical World*—and will be again performed entire at the approaching Liverpool festival in October, by which time the pianoforte score of the whole oratorio, arranged by the author, the separate vocal parts and the separate orchestral parts will be ready for delivery to those who may favour J. A. N. with their orders." The pianoforte score was published at thirty-two shillings, or in two parts sixteen shillings each, the

---

author of another compilation called "Sacred Melodies," and of the works entitled "The Music of Nature" and "Music and Friends." It is asserted that the chamber music of Beethoven was first performed in this country at his house.

vocal parts at five shillings each. The books 1 and 3 of the "Lieder ohne Worte," or Songs without Words, had been published previously.*

This work, which was the most noteworthy publication of the year, was the first new oratorio of its dimensions given forth within the century. Upon its success the fortunes of the house of Novello were built, and the spirit of enterprise involved in the matter guided and directed all future transactions in which the house engaged.

---

* The first book was originally published, for the author, under the title of " Original Melodies for the Pianoforte."

J. ALFRED NOVELLO.

CHAPTER I.

1837—1847.

"Train'd in music."—*Pericles*, Act iv., Sc. 1.

IN the year 1837, when Queen Victoria ascended the throne of her ancestors, music was not in the most flourishing or happy condition.

A long period of neglect had deprived native art of that freedom which is essential to an active and progressive exercise. The chief exponents of the divine science—not then, be it said, fully admitted to the privileges it should enjoy as a science, for it was not freely acknowledged as such—were alternately petted or despised, according as their services were required, or their occasional attempts to assert their position as citizens obtruded upon the notice of the leaders of society. The love for music was general, and widely spread among all classes. The actual knowledge of its principles and practice was limited in amount, and restricted to a very few. The practice of music in private life was rare, and its cultivation in the domestic circle somewhat apologetic. The chief show piece on the pianoforte was still the "Battle of Prague," or "The Linnet Waltz," written "by somebody and dedicated to everybody." Music was not cultivated for its own sake, but for some relative association. The flute was a favourite instrument with gentlemen who desired to be thought musical, because it was convenient and portable, and suited well with the dismal bearing affected by those with a turn for romance. Byron, be it remembered, was the favourite poet. Some young ladies practised the guitar as a *genteel* kind of instrument. Others preferred the harp, especially those with elegant hands, arms, and feet. Duets and trios were constructed upon an ingenious plan. They required two or three voices to execute them properly, as their respective titles implied, but each part was chiefly restricted to the delivery of alternate solos, and when the voices were brought together, the harmony was so arranged that it did not suffer if it was left out altogether; the voices often sang the air in unison, and left the harmony entirely to the accompanist. The art of glee singing proper, however, was much cultivated by professional musicians, some of whom were writers of glees, and all of whom preserved the right traditions. There were also several private societies maintained by subscription for the practice and performance of glee singing.

Pianoforte playing was not studied to the extent it is now. It was a rare thing indeed to find a gentleman capable of playing even a few chords upon the instrument, notwithstanding the fact that good examples had been set by young Sterndale Bennett, Cipriani Potter, then the two famous native soloists, and J. W. Davison, the most skilful and sympathetic accompanist of the time. The pianoforte was an instrument best *fitted for the use of ladies.* *

On the Continent Liszt had already revolutionised

---

* The manly undergraduates of Oxford at this period actually hissed a male pianist off the stage of the Star Assembly Rooms, for undertaking what they considered to be a duty which should have been left to the other sex.

the musical world by his playing, but his influence had not yet been felt in England. He was only looked upon as a prodigy, not as a reformer.

Pianoforte solos were rare even in the best concerts, popular taste running in favour of vocal music. When a performer like Thalberg did appear, he played Fantasias and Variations rather than Sonatas or Concertos. Dexterity of execution was the goal sought alike by players and singers. Floridity of style was the rule. Each player or vocalist endeavoured to outvie his colleagues in the ingenuity of his *fioriture* or his *bravura* singing. "We have but to repeat the same terms of admiration at M. Thalberg's playing. It is as refined as it is wonderful. After going through his herculean task (and the fantasia he played contains the most enormous of his difficulties) he acknowledged the enthusiasm and encore of his audience by playing the fantasia in which he introduces variations upon 'God save the King,' and 'Rule, Britannia.' The room was in an uproar." This was at a Philharmonic Concert. The musical critics of the time favoured the habit of florid execution and vocalisation, and in this manner urged its observance.

Speaking of the singing of Grisi and Albertazzi, we read in the *Atlas*, "The latter lady is beginning to set scholastic precision in its proper place, making it subservient to the genius of melody, in which she revels more discursively than formerly; but she can yet afford to infuse into her style more impulse."

The want of "impulse" was lamented in more matters than the singing of a *prima donna*. Those who looked forward to the future hoped for a more satisfactory state of things than that which existed, and none laboured more strenuously to this end than Alfred Novello, supported by his worthy father. There were many hindrances, the chief being found in the firmly rooted prejudices of all classes, and the pertinacity with which they were retained, and their existence defended. However great might be the desire to create an "impulse" which should be useful in its effects, sufficient power had not accumulated, and difficulties increased as the days grew on. The popular love for music had never been denied, but means for popular education did not exist. The people had little or no legislative power. Their wants were known only to themselves, for the higher classes took no interest in the desires of the poor. It is true that men's minds were shaken with the strong breeze of Reform which was then blowing over the land. The hoped-for reform was chiefly to be relied upon to affect many existing abuses, and only indirectly to institute changes which might benefit the community. Music could never be thoroughly popular until it was within the reach of all. True art lingered in fretful captivity under mere fashionable patronage. The people longed to give it welcome on their own hearths. The restrictions which surrounded it kept it away from those who could value it for its own sake, and for the refining influence a better knowledge of it would bring. There were no cheap publications, and there were no cheap concerts. The taxes on knowledge and the vexatious rules observed by the printing trades laid an embargo upon all attempts at reform in this direction.

"The drama's laws the drama's patrons give," and

while the stage yielded to popular wishes, music remained almost inflexible to outside influences.

The Sacred Harmonic Society, which in later years was enabled to do much for the advancement of choral music, was then an infant association, established in 1832—small in number of members—meeting in an unpretending out of the way place for mutual instruction and practice in Handel's works. A performance of "The Messiah" in aid of a charity had been one of the most important efforts of the society in the year 1836, and in the Spring of the year 1837 (6th March), Mendelssohn's "St. Paul" was performed by this body for the first time in London, and repeated on the 12th September in the presence of the composer. For this the services of nearly five hundred performers were enlisted. This was the Popular Society.

The Philharmonic Society, established in 1813 by Vincent Novello, Attwood, Sir George Smart, Horsley, Bishop, Salomon, Ayrton, Cramer, Clementi, Corri, Dance, and others, was supported chiefly by musicians, formed into two classes—members and associates.

The support of the Antient Concerts was restricted to persons of rank, and the privilege of membership was eagerly sought after. The spirit of reform shook their foundations, and, yielding to the force of circumstances, they finally faded out of existence after having fulfilled their mission. They had been established some sixty years at the beginning of the Queen's reign, but their chief work was accomplished, and they were soon to cease to exist.

These Antient Concerts were founded in 1776,

and up to 1795 they were given in the New Rooms in Tottenham Street, afterwards known as "The Queen's" or West London Theatre. Subsequently the performances took place at the Concert Room of the Opera House; and, when transferred to the Hanover Square Rooms in 1804, were held there until 1848.

The principle upon which the royal and noble founders of the institution acted was to give no music by living composers. This ultra-conservative idea was intended to check the waywardness of modern ideas. It was thought—no doubt wisely— that "the *good* that men do lives after them." Therefore the admission of a work by any composer in the programmes would only be granted twenty years after his death. The subscribers had to wait for over thirty years after the death of Mozart before his name appeared in the programmes. The only exception made was in the case of Beethoven, for a piece of music by him was heard by the society in 1835, eight years after his death. The director for the day fixed the programmes. The last director was the Duke of Wellington, in 1848, the year in which the society came to an end. It was killed by the too rigid pursuance of the principles which called it into being. It had grown too exclusive for a world in which all things are progressive. When the tide is at ebb no changes appear to be going on. When it is at flood, things that were apparently stationary and solid are either swamped or swept away. Those who move not with the caravan are left to perish in the desert.

The Italian Opera was the chief fashionable form

of entertainment, and like the Antient Concerts, and the meetings of the Philharmonic Society, offered few attractions to the ordinary amateurs. The privileges of these institutions were jealously guarded, and the general public was only admitted to participate in the pleasures they offered, as it were, on sufferance. The idea of catering for the people outside the circle was beyond the thoughts, as it certainly was beyond the practice, of the directors of the higher forms of musical entertainments. There were very few other public concerts and few public halls. Hanover Square Rooms, Willis's Rooms, the Old Argyll Rooms, Regent Street, the Music Hall in Store Street, Bedford Square, and a few assembly rooms in old fashioned taverns, were all that were available. Away from the Philharmonic Society, or the so-called Oratorios at the two Patent theatres, in Drury Lane and Covent Garden, during the season of Lent, little orchestral music of an elevating character could be heard.

Composers wrote for small orchestras not always complete, and did not in every case strive to court attention by instrumental colouring. Those like Bishop, Balfe, Barnett, Hullah, and others—then before the public—were not unmindful of the general fancy, and wrote melodiously. Operas were estimated according to the provender they contained for Mr. Weippert and his quadrilles.

While the music in the theatres and the public halls was arranged ostensibly with a view to elevate the taste of that section of the public which was assumed to possess more or less knowledge, the ignorant and the easily pleased were also provided with the means supposed to be within their powers of appreciation. There were concerts given in public houses, on what was called the "Free and Easy" principle; that is to say, the programmes, generally *impromptu*, were either made up entirely from, or were largely indebted to, the efforts of the visitors, on the voluntary system. A pianist was engaged who "vamped" accompaniments to the songs performed, which were always sung by ear, even by the so-called professional vocalists. These "professionals" were not always qualified by high education. Some of them could scarcely read or write, yet not a few were the composers of songs—words and music—which enjoyed a considerable amount of popularity. The "professional" augmented his stock-in-trade by making occasional visits to the better class of concert room, where his position was recognised and secured him free admission. He listened to the new songs, and retaining them in his memory, retailed them to his patrons. If his songs "took," they sometimes found their way into the penny song-books used by those who frequented establishments honoured by his association. The verses were taken down by the editors of these publications from the dictation of those who had caught them up by ear, and not unfrequently words of similar sound, not always consonant with the sense, were substituted for the correct ones. These "free and easy" concert rooms supplied a popular form of entertainment, but there was not sufficient interest in them to secure continuous support. The "rooms" were only opened two, or at the most three, nights a week, and the "professionals," who depended upon them for a living, wandered from one to another, to find a temple for the exercise of their avocations.

The popular love for music had an existence, though "it was born and nurtured through the poverty of ignorance." The standard of taste not being very high among the people, the absence of discriminating power among audiences in general gave rise to careless and even to bad work in what were supposed to be high class performances. Singers and performers who had been well trained, instead of persistently endeavouring to elevate the popular judgment, drifted into ways of indifference, and, counting upon the ignorance of those before whom they performed, made false taste serve as the true canon of art.

When Lablache first came to London he attended the rehearsals at the theatre, and, being a zealous and conscientious artist, he was disgusted at the inartistic tricks played by his fellow performers and asked to be released from his engagement. He was persuaded to wait, and when he had made his *début* he altered his mind, and said, "When I see the public applauding everything that is in bad taste, I perceive and admit that my brethren are in the right not to do better."

An attempt made to form an organised *Claque* by some of the members of the Parisian fraternity was defeated, although it was seriously stated and believed that the introduction of applause in the proper place would tend to the improvement of the judgment of audiences in general. There was no need to force the public into an appreciation of good music. Unscientific as audiences of the time were, educational advantages were not withheld. Many young musicians, George Macfarren—or McFarran, as they spelt his name sometimes—John Hullah, not yet the apostle of popular musical knowledge, William Sterndale Bennett, and others were hard at work to show practically the need of higher elevation.

Some of the newspaper critics of the time, in the intervals occupied by personal abuse or good humoured banter directed against caterers for the public, found time to preach in favour of cheap popular entertainments. The Sacred Harmonic Society had shown that grand musical effects "were no longer to be sought exclusively in the provincial festivals." The lowest price of a ticket for the society's concerts was three shillings, and this provision of popular oratorios" was gladly hailed as "a cheap enjoyment for the multitudes of the most unquestionable character, a diffusion of the refinement of taste, and a power of appreciation, which belong to the best agencies of civilisation." They were in fact, though not in form, a mission for elevating the taste, and by that for elevating the moral improvement of the middle classes of society.

Cheaper performances were not thought possible, for the thought of cheap music had scarcely entered men's minds. The step taken by Alfred Novello, in the publication of his "Cheap Classics," was certainly on the right track, but the path was beset with obstacles which could only be gradually removed. The task of clearing the road was undertaken and continued with singleness of purpose all through his business life. As a singer, engaged in the performance of these "popular oratorios" in London and in the provinces, he had intimate means of making himself acquainted with popular needs. These he endeavoured to supply in his capacity as a publisher.

The history of the house during the ten years which began with the publication of "St. Paul," embraced many important events affecting the cause of music. Besides the works already spoken of as having been published by the firm, then represented by Alfred Novello, the Masses of Haydn and Mozart, other music for the Roman Catholic Church, the splendid edition of Purcell, and Boyce's Collection of Cathedral Music — organ part and vocal parts (1842)—for the use of the Anglican Church, appeared, and were followed by publications for the use of choirs of all denominations. The publication of some of the Psalms in 1837-40 and the Lobgesang in 1841-2 by Mendelssohn, the latter with English words adapted by Alfred Novello, and the first English Edition of Rossini's "Stabat Mater,"* was also a most important step in the history of Art. There were then few small works available for the use of Choral Societies and these were most eagerly welcomed. Novello's Choral Hand Book, which contained a few simple Anthems in use in the Cathedral service, brought those works within the reach of other choirs. They were published in separate parts at threepence per page. Nothing cheaper

---

* The "Stabat Mater" was first sung in England at the Catholic Chapel, Old London Road, in 1841, Cecilia Novello (Mrs. Serle) taking the soprano solos.

had ever appeared before. A large number of other Anthems was issued in like fashion, in obedience to the demand created by the revival of Church feeling in and about the year 1840.

Mainzer's many publications, including "Singing for the Million," which phrase was taken by Hood as the subject of a humorous poem, were issued by the house. The choruses of Mainzer's composition or selection were published at one penny each, "marvellously cheap." These were eagerly taken up and studied by the labourers in the many workshops throughout the length and breadth of the land.

Alfred Novello's commercial tours were exalted into the dignity of musical missions. His knowledge of music and wide-minded sympathies constituted his authority in cases of appeal or advice. His cheap publications had made the formation of Choral Societies possible. In the large factories of Yorkshire and Lancashire many Choral Unions existed, and the publications of the house were gladly welcomed, because of their modest price and their perfect accuracy. The publisher in his progress was always cordially received, and often concerts were given in his honour, the performers making extra exertions to show their advancement since his last visit. The cause thus received its greatest help from Alfred Novello, not only by his valuable and useful publications, but by his personal influence.

In 1841 Mr. Henry Littleton's connection with the house began by his entering into Mr. Novello's service in a subordinate position. His extraordinary business capacity, grasp of detail, and general strength of character were soon recognised, and, starting from the lowest round of the ladder, in three years he attained a position only second to the head of the firm. Many of the enterprising transactions of the house were due to the shrewdness of his judgment, power of will, and untiring industry.

The sisters, Cecilia, Clara, and Sabilla Novello, then prominently before the public either as singers or as teachers, also assisted directly and indirectly to further the love for music revived in the hearts of the people, and to augment the fortunes of the house, by bringing its publications into notice. This valuable form of help, highly appreciated by Alfred Novello, together with his own exertions as a vocalist, mitigated the cost of advertisement, which in those days was burthened with a heavy duty, and was oppressed by a capricious mode of estimating the amount. This was only one among the many vexatious taxes upon knowledge. Some of them, imposed in the reign of Queen Anne, were originally intended to secure accuracy of information, and to facilitate methods of tracing authorship, but had grown into harassing obstructions in the way of the march of intellect. Every publication which contained any item of news must bear a stamp; every advertisement must pay a duty to the Government. There was also a heavy excise duty on paper, and an import duty on books and music. Perhaps the most irritating of the taxes on knowledge were found in the trade rules of the printers. Continuous efforts, strenuously made, might in time induce the Government to yield to the demand for a free and unfettered press, but only the determined action of a few capitalists who had found a market for their goods could break down the rules of the trade—rules which kept men idle at times, and often deprived them of bread. The press, as an instrument of enlightenment, was not fulfilling all its functions, because the workers hindered the power of development by their self-imposed restrictions. Improvements in printing were discouraged in order to keep up the cost of labour; consequently the public derived no advantage. Sheet music was printed direct from the engraved plates, which were worn out after a certain number of impressions had been taken off. Messrs. Clowes, the famous printers, had effected considerable improvements in type music printing; but the trades union rules for compositors made their method almost useless. The cost of setting up the words in connection with music type was nearly double that of the like measurement of words or letters when standing alone. The transfer of plate impressions of music pages to lithographic stones was not then perfectly understood, and the possibility of further cheapening the cost of music seemed to be more remote than ever.*

---

* Carl Maria von Weber was one of the first who employed lithography for the purposes of music-printing. His early compositions were printed from lithographic stones, to save the expense of plates, after the process invented by Aloys Senefelder, an actor in his father's company. Both father and son practised the art, and attained considerable skill in it. The son, in fact, daunted by the failure of his first compositions, had abandoned music for a time in favour of lithography. When in 1804, the year when "Rübezahl" was written, music once more asserted its fascinations, Weber nearly lost his life by drinking some nitric acid used for lithographic purposes. The bottle containing the fluid had been left on the table by mistake by his father, and Weber, wearied and exhausted, thinking it was wine, drank some of the contents. His mouth and windpipe were burnt, and his illness lasted for more than two months. He recovered under the efforts of his medical attendants, but his voice was gone, and never recovered its full power.

The Octavo Editions.

When *The Musical Times* was projected, in 1844, the printer could not afford to break through the rules of the trade for so small a quantity of work as the issue of the paper promised. This caused Alfred Novello, as will be seen later, to enter upon the new business of type music printer himself. He would not abandon an undertaking which he foresaw would be of immense value in popularising music and helping the fulfilment of his cherished scheme, the reduction of the taxes on knowledge. He thus became an "outside the trade" printer, who could only get the help of non-unionist workmen, but his spirited enterprise effected a considerable revolution. The trades union relaxed its rule after three years' obstinate resistance. The Messrs. Clowes had in the meantime threatened to destroy their splendid fount of music type, as rendered useless by the old trade rules. One provoking law having been broken down, other customs were disregarded. It was now found to be possible to produce a readable page of music in an octavo size, suitable for use by performers at a concert, available as text-books by audiences, and a cheap book of reference at all times.

The idea of the "Octavo Editions" had its origin in the size selected for *The Musical Times*. The object in issuing the publication was chiefly to encourage the formation of choral societies, to record their progress, and to provide material for practice in the class. "All communications of the progress of singing-class teaching" were invited to be sent to the editor. The publication consisted of eight pages, three or four containing a piece of music, and the rest musical news and advertisements.

The price was three-halfpence. This sum was, and still is, charged for the music alone when separated from the periodical.

Meantime the list of Anthems, &c., published in separate parts, was increasing; and a city house was established in May, 1845, at No. 24, Poultry, at the sign of "The Golden Crotchet,"* for the convenience of musical people in the city. Choral societies for the improvement of singing in churches were established in London, and to meet the ever-increasing demand for the works of the old church writers, a new edition of "Boyce's *own* Services and Anthems," edited by Vincent Novello, published by subscription, was issued in two volumes, at sixteen shillings each; the number of the subscribers amounting to nearly 400. The whole series formed four volumes. The first and second were "a reprint" of the edition by Philip Hayes; the third and fourth contained Services and Anthems by Boyce never before collected. The separate organ part was added by Novello.

At the end of the year 1845, the "Surrey Chapel Music," as performed at the then most famous of all the dissenting places of worship, was proposed to be published in sixteen numbers, at one shilling each, with the organ or pianoforte part added by Vincent Novello. Two hundred and fifty subscribers only were required to justify the publisher in his outlay.

The title of "Sacred Music Warehouse" had been occasionally used in connection with 69, Dean Street, but now the house assumed a new title, that of "The London Sacred Music Warehouse," 69, Dean Street, Soho, and 24, Poultry.

---

* This was one of the last of the London signs.

Cheap Edition of "The Messiah." 35

In January, 1846, Mr. Edward Holmes became associated with *The Musical Times*, and his contributions gave a literary tone to the publication, which had not been aimed at before.* Two months later the issue of a reprint of Beethoven's Mass in D, in time for the famous Philharmonic performance in the following May, was announced—"Pianoforte Score, price twenty-one shillings." Beethoven's Mass had been published some years before, when no one ever thought of performing it, and when even musicians of advanced ideas thought it impracticable. So far was the house in advance of the times.

In July, 1846, there appeared the following significant advertisement :—

The cheapest Musical Publication ever offered to the public,
in respect both to quality and quantity ! ! ! "

" Handel's Sacred Oratorio
'THE MESSIAH'
in Vocal Score
With separate accompaniment for the Organ or Pianoforte
Arranged by
VINCENT NOVELLO."

---

* Edward Holmes, born 1797, died August 28, 1859, was a pupil of Vincent Novello. He wrote "A Ramble among the Musicians of Germany," 1828 ; a "Life of Mozart," 1845, still among the best biographies existing ; and a "Life of Purcell" for the second issue of Novello's edition of Purcell's Sacred Music; an Analytical and Thematic Index of Mozart's Pianoforte Works; Analyses of Mozart's Masses, written for and printed in *The Musical Times*, &c. His wife was a granddaughter of Samuel Webbe, the composer.

D 2

"The whole work will be complete in Twelve monthly numbers, price sixpence each. To commence on the first of August, 1846."* †

In the number of *The Musical Times* for August the chorus " And he shall purify " is given as a specimen of the new edition of "The Messiah." The complete copy cost six shillings and sixpence. The success of the publication soon brought forth another, Haydn's "Creation," issued and completed in nine sixpenny numbers. In like manner were published "Judas Maccabæus," "Jephtha," "St. Paul," and other works, besides a goodly list of musical publications for the "Established Church of Great Britain and Ireland," as it was then. A large number of Psalmody books, with reminiscences of eighteenth century titles: "Miriam's Timbrel," "Harmonia Sacra," "Cantica Sacra," "Melodia Sacra," for the use of dissenters; Collections of Chants, &c., a subscription edition of Croft's Anthems, in two volumes, price twenty shillings each, with a long list of glees and secular pieces,

---

* With one or two exceptions, every Oratorio that Handel wrote is now included in the series of Cheap Oratorios published by the firm—forming the most lasting and universal monument that has ever been erected to the memory of the composer.

† Alfred Novello paid thirty pounds for an advertisement in the *Illustrated London News* of the prospectus, containing a specimen page of this edition of "The Messiah." The advertisement was accepted and a receipt given, but the money was returned, because the specimen page could not be inserted, as it might offend their patrons; and, moreover, it was against the principles of the paper to insert "blocks" not of their own making. These principles have since been submitted to revision, as the heterogeneous nature of the advertisements which are now allowed to appear would seem to show.

testified to the growing importance of the house. Success had not been attained without anxiety and trouble. Twice had the printer of the music type been changed, because of the demands of the compositors' trades union.

It was in February, 1847, that Alfred Novello began as a printer. He had long been active in the endeavour to obtain the removal of the taxes upon knowledge, and had in fact acted as treasurer to the society formed for the purpose. To his already great responsibilities, he now added another, which was better calculated to secure his end. He could only employ "non-union" men, but, free from harassing restrictions, he could carry out many plans for the furtherance of his design to popularise music, without fear or favour. The means by which the trade sought to ruin him became the foundation of his prosperity. With greater freedom came greater endeavours. The change of feeling in all artistic matters at the time, which arose out of the endeavour to repair the errors of the past, prompted men to begin anew as from the date when the departure from integrity was assumed to have taken place, and a quaint spirit of mediævalism arose. This was exhibited in painting by the works of the so-called Pre-Raphaelites; and in printing by a re-introduction of founts of type which had been set aside as old-fashioned. Where the matrices existed the types were re-cast, and new dies of like pattern were cut to supply the sizes which modern ingenuity had introduced since the old styles had been disused. A considerable number of inconsistencies had been imported with these "restorations," among others certain peculiarities of spelling, which were considered appropriate, or that at all events served to minister to the passing fancy.

The proverb, "It is better to be out of the world than out of the fashion," seems to have guided Mr. Novello when, at the outset of his new career, he published a small pamphlet, giving "Some account of the Method of Musick Printing, with specimens of the various sizes of Moveable Types; and of other matters. Imprinted by J. Alfred Novello, Dean's Yard, over against Dean Street, near Soho Square, in the City of Westminster." In this he informs his friends and patrons that "he has latterly organised a Printing-house for the production of works in typography in general, and more especially for such as require moveable music types. The cheap and popular editions of the oratorios which are now in course of publication may be cited as creditable specimens of his workmanship. In addition to the type used for these oratorios, he can undertake to print in larger sized founts." Then follow specimens of five music founts which he had lately added to his already ample stock. The punches for two of these founts, the pearl nonpareil and the gem gregorian, had been cut expressly and at considerable cost, for his own use, and were remarkable for their boldness and clearness. The pamphlet also contained a short sketch of "The Economics of Musick Printing," setting forth the merits of the two methods employed —*viz.*, pewter plates and moveable types; and advising intending publishers as to the method most suitable to their work.

Soon afterwards the "gem," the fount used at the

present time for the octavo editions, was designed, and the work of cutting the punches undertaken by Mr. Palmer of the Soho Type Foundry. This fount was intended to be a great improvement upon the music types then in use, and no pains or expense were spared to make it so. Experience had shown that new combinations and characters could be used with advantage, and many of these were cut for the new fount. The work being of a special character, and extremely difficult and expensive in its execution, took about six years to complete, and it was not till 1853-4 that the first fount was delivered in Dean's Yard. Many additions and improvements have since then been made, and others are now in progress, which when completed will add still more to the beauty and clearness of the works in which they are employed. With his new old-fashioned type the literary portion of *The Musical Times* was now printed, and with the new " Musick Types" a notable improvement was effected in the compositions given with each number. So soon as the son of Vincent Novello, that great pioneer of cheap music, was enabled to start as a printer on his own account, forced into that responsibility by the restrictions of the trade laws conceived and maintained in a spirit totally opposed to the theory of the duties of the press, he made the attempt to introduce reforms in the ways and habits of his new business.

The plan (commenced in the first number) of giving music with sacred words in the even numbers, and secular music in the odd numbers, was kept up for a considerable time. At the present day each yearly volume contains six pieces of music set to words of sacred import, and a like number to words of secular character.

This arrangement gave general satisfaction to the numerous singing classes. They were enabled to acquire at a very cheap rate a series of works which, by their variety, imparted a charm to the weekly meetings beyond that which arose from the following of a fashionable inclination.

Musicians also approved of the work done, as will appear from the following extract from an extended notice of the first six numbers of *The Musical Times*, which appeared in *The Musical World*. The new work is called "a very unpretending publication, but one of considerable merit and utility. Each number contains an article of first rate interest—generally an essay on some important musical composition—and miscellaneous paragraphs on passing topics of the day. But the principal feature is a composition in vocal score—a glee, madrigal, or chorus, as the case may be—adapted peculiarly to the singing classes now so much in vogue. Purcell, Winter, Festa, Weber, Beethoven, Novello, Spofforth, &c., have already been drawn upon. The price of the work (three-halfpence) leaves us no cause for surprise at the circulation which it has already attained — a circulation, we believe, little short of three thousand. The work appears on the first day of every month, and is fully worth the attention of the members of choral societies, for whom it is especially intended, and for those musicians who would possess a cheap and correct edition of some of the choice works of the greatest vocal writers."

American Agencies.

One of the last acts of the year 1847 was the announcement of Gottfried Weber's "Theory of Musical Composition," translated by James F. Warner, of Boston, America. The copies were merely imported, but as one of the earliest of the musical literary works issued by the firm, its publication is significant, and closes an eventful period. The anticipations of the wants of the people in the matter of music for the sustenance of the many singing classes which had sprung up in all parts, had created fresh needs among the ranks for whom such provision was made. The growth of the interest in the matter was not confined to Great Britain alone, but had extended itself to the Colonies and the Continent of America. In Boston and in New York direct agencies had been established; and almost for the first time in the history of a British music publishing house, the names of American firms directly in communication with the London house were printed upon the catalogues, and upon certain of the publications. Thus unity of feeling upon questions of the spread of knowledge was shown to exist between peoples springing from the same stock, politically severed, but now artistically re-united.

The catalogue of the publications of the house which, at the beginning of the Queen's reign, was comprised within very narrow limits, at the end of the year 1847 occupied a volume of 130 pages. It was divided into six sections:—
No. 1. Organ Music, comprising specially written pieces, arrangements, and adaptations. No. 2. Sacred Music with English words, comprising services,

anthems, hymns, songs and solo hymns, duets and trios, psalmody, Purcell's sacred music, oratorios, cantatas and large psalms, collections of sacred music, cheap musical classics, and so forth. No. 3. Separate Vocal and Instrumental Parts for Church Choirs, Singing Classes, and Choral Societies. In this list we find oratorios, cantatas, anthems, and large psalms, single choruses, English church services, anthems, Latin music, overtures in separate parts, &c. This, one of the older forms of the catalogue, was published partly by arrangement with Mr. Surman, of Exeter Hall, then conductor of the Sacred Harmonic Society, the list containing some of his publications, mingled with the copyrights of Alfred Novello. No. 4. Instrumental works for the pianoforte, solo and duet; flute music, a specialty; music for the flageolet and pianoforte, guitar, harp, violin, and violoncello, together with a few elementary treatises on the science of music and of different instruments, such as Miss Elliott's "Elementary Compendium," the Abbé O'Donelly's "Academy of Elementary Music," Goodban's "Pack of fifty-two Music Cards, with book of directions for playing a variety of instructive and entertaining games on the rudimental principles of the science of music"; Schneider's work on the organ; Coggins, Goodban, and Reinagle on the pianoforte; Chipp on the harp; Kirkman and Horetzky on the guitar; Parado's and Ribas's Studies and Scales for the flute; Hyde on the trumpet, and Hunt on the cornet-à-pistons; excellent works in their day which have had to yield to later improvements. No. 5. An enumeration of songs, duets, glees, and madrigals, with English, Italian,

French, German, and other words, including songs with guitar accompaniment. Both the guitar and the flute retained their popularity as household instruments forty years ago. No. 6. The last catalogue in the list was "Sacred Music with Latin Words."

From this time forth the catalogue assumed a more cosmopolitan character, and the idea with which the business was commenced—namely, that of supplying cheap music — was to receive a most vigorous expansion at the outset of the next decade in the history of the house.

CHAPTER II.

1848—1857.

" What fine change is in the music."
Two Gentlemen of Verona, Act iv., Sc. 2.

THE course of the progress of a house of business can be best traced by reference to the surrounding circumstances which contributed directly or indirectly to its advancement.

From the date of the first publications of Vincent Novello, one spirit animated all concerned, one object was kept firmly in view. This was to try and discover what was needed for the advancement of musical art, and to make the best endeavours to supply it in a manner conformable to the need. The cultivation of the habit of looking out for what was to come enabled the watcher to direct men's minds into the proper channel, so far as he possessed the power. Long before any serious effort was made to nationalise the practice and study of music, by the classes instituted by John Hullah, with the countenance, if not with the more substantial support of the Privy Council, attempts had been made to establish classes for teaching the elements of music. Hickson's classes are spoken of as early as the year 1839, the year Joseph Mainzer came to England. At the same time that John Hullah was working with the Wilhem system, Mainzer, who had successfully instituted classes for music and singing among the workmen in Paris, started his "Singing for the Million" in London, and enjoyed a considerable share of success.

Mainzer's classes were at first chiefly supported by the advocates of temperance. The study of music and the establishment of singing classes were strongly advocated by philanthropists, in the hope that by these means the lower classes might be weaned from drunkenness and dissipation. The famous Father Matthew, the apostle of temperance as he was called, recommended music as an antidote to the moral poison of drink, and he even invited Mainzer to Ireland, with a view to establishing vocal associations in that part of the kingdom. Sir Richard Mayne, formerly Chief Commissioner of Police, asserted that the extension of permission for musical performances in public houses led to a considerable diminution in the statistics of drunkenness and crime.

At the commencement of the period upon which entrance is now being made—namely, the second decade in the reign of the Queen, from 1848 to 1857—*The Musical Times* had expanded its original eight pages into twelve. The enlargement commenced with the February number in 1848. The publisher states, "That the sale of copies has now reached so large a number as to make *The Musical Times* by far the best medium for the diffusion of musical information of a temporary nature, or for the announcement of forthcoming works."

The cheap edition of "St. Paul," "to be completed in twelve monthly numbers, sixteen pages, in a neat wrapper, price sixpence"; with "Judas Maccabæus," No 8, price sixpence; " Cathedral Choir Book," No. 7, folio, organ score, one shilling and sixpence:

8vo, vocal score, one shilling; 8vo, vocal parts, fourpence each, with *The Musical Times*, were the current monthly musical publications of the house, whose spirited action seemed to be founded on Virgil's words, " Audentes fortuna juvat."

At this time Mr. Surman, a music publisher with whom Alfred Novello had large dealings, was removed from his office as conductor of the Sacred Harmonic Society. It appears that he entertained a disagreeable feeling in consequence of his removal, and with short-sighted policy threw hindrances in the way of fair trade. Novello was temporarily unable to supply his customers according to their orders, but, undaunted, he set to work with characteristic energy, and found a means to overcome the difficulty and to increase the usefulness of his own publications. To his customers, and to the public, he issued a letter in which he craved the indulgence of his patrons, while he employed men to furnish the plates for the printing of the works so churlishly withheld by Mr. Surman: " I have tried to send you the music you want by transferring your order to other London musicsellers, but with no success; and you will readily understand that all must be denied, or the society (the Sacred Harmonic) could not be prevented from buying the parts they may want. I have taken immediate steps to repair this temporary inconvenience by engraving the whole of the parts, which I have been induced to advertise in my catalogue, and considerable progress is already made with them; but as it is unavoidably a work requiring time, my friends, I hope, will have a little patience with me. I will, however, use all diligence, and I can promise them that they shall not long be deprived of the power of purchasing parts, even if Mr. Surman should not awaken to a sense of what he owes to the public who have hitherto supported him. The present unexpected course of Mr. Surman is not altogether without its public advantage, for I am in a manner forced to undertake the printing of these parts, which I should not otherwise have done; and I am thereby enabled to introduce all those improvements which have been so much required."

The new editions of these vocal and instrumental parts were not only improved in appearance and in accuracy, but, as will be seen later, they were sold at a considerably lower price than heretofore.

The growing interest in Gregorian music called forth a series of adaptations of the modes, and of services, hymns, and psalms "usually chanted in choirs at vespers and complin." Handel's Oratorio "Jephtha" was the new serial work, and Dr. S. S. Wesley's Psalter, or Psalms of David with Chants, "in the mode universally adopted in the Church of England," is announced, together with a new edition of a large collection of the older standard hymn tunes —the Surrey Chapel Psalmody.

"The Norwich Sol-fa Ladder," price threepence. Jarrold and Son, 47, St. Paul's Churchyard, London, is advertised in the August number of *The Musical Times* in 1848. This belonged to Miss Glover's Tetrachordal method, the precursor of the Tonic Sol-fa notation, into which, thirty years later, so many of the publications of the firm were translated.

A folio edition of "The Messiah," in vocal score, with an accompaniment for the organ or pianoforte, by Vincent Novello, "price only ten shillings," was also announced. For this edition of "The Messiah" the beautiful "pearl-nonpareil" music-type, which was cast for Alfred Novello, was employed, and *a large-sized type* was made expressly for the words.

The Musical Times becomes naturally the medium by which the progress of the house can be traced. In several of the numbers of this year, 1848, the advertisements of the publications of C. Coventry, No. 71, Dean Street, appear, and in the November number, Messrs. Ewer and Co., 72, Newgate Street, advertise several vocal and instrumental works by various composers, Mendelssohn's "Elijah" among others. In later days these two firms were to be absorbed by the house of Novello, though, probably, no thought of the kind at that time entered the minds of the head of the firm, or of his then indispensable and indefatigable assistant, Mr. Henry Littleton.

The matter which really occupied their minds was not the absorption of firms in which any shadow of rivalry existed, but how to increase legitimately the business which had been made so extensively useful by their exertions. Already the cheap music of the house of Novello had called classes and societies into existence which, but for the aid they furnished, could have had no being. Music was apparently as cheap as attendant circumstances would permit; and, considering all things, there were no means by which the publisher could gain a profit on his undertaking, if he were, in defiance of custom, to lessen the percentage required on his outlay. Alfred Novello was a man of reflective and thoughtful turn of mind, and he had seen how the income and the business of the Post Office had been increased by the reduction of the rates of postage. But whether this thought occurred to his mind or not, on the first day of the new year, 1849, he issued the following circular, addressed to the musical public :—

"Tidings do I bring, and lucky joys,
And golden times, and happy news of price."
Henry IV., Part 2.
" Make trivial price of serious things."
All's well that ends well.

"The reasons which have determined J. Alfred Novello to reduce the price of his musical publications, the majority of them to the full extent of fifty per cent.

"During the last twenty years there has been a progressive increase in the culture of music. In the earlier part of this period classical works were published only with great sacrifice on the part of the printer, and the demand for such works was so limited that the cost of engraving, printing, and payment to the composer was obliged to be divided among a small number of copies, and this small number took many years to sell.

" Many works were thus placed within the reach of amateurs which had previously been confined to the libraries of the few, and this facility tended much to *increase* the musical taste which it was intended to supply. Gradually classical music was produced in greater abundance, but still the cost was obliged to be divided on the probable sale of but very few copies.

"It may not be amiss, by a few figures, more fully

Reduced Prices.

to explain the difficulty a publisher labours under when printing a book for which he can expect but few buyers; and in the second statement it will be seen how he can afford to sell the same book at a lower price, if he can calculate upon a larger sale.

"We will suppose—

The cost of the *copyright*, or payment to the author...	£10	10	0
The cost of plates, engraving, &c.... ...	10	0	0
The cost of printing and paper for 200 copies	15	0	0
	£35	10	0

"This expense divided amongst 200 purchasers is three shillings and sixpence each.

"But suppose a larger number of purchasers—

The cost to the *author*, and of *engraving*, &c., as before	£20	10	0
The cost of *printing* and *paper* for 2,000 copies, same rate as before	150	0	0
	£170	10	0

"Expense divided among 2,000 purchasers is about one shilling and ninepence each.

"The advance made in the culture of classical music within the last few years of the period just mentioned has so much multiplied the buyers of the better class of music, that it has induced the experiments which I have been making by the publication of *Oratorios* and *Church music* at prices which could only repay the first outlay by the sale of numerous copies. On a careful consideration of the altered state of musical taste, and the success of the late experiments, *two questions* of some moment have arisen—viz., first, whether the majority of the works I print might not be reduced in price with advantage to the public and the advancement of musical taste, and still with safety to myself? and, *secondly*, how far such reduction would be just to those who have purchased these works at the prices hitherto charged?

"The *first question*, after mature consideration, I have thought should be decided in the affirmative, for although the reduction of the prices (in most instances full fifty per cent.) will entail much the same risk as that incurred by the earlier editions of classical music, yet it may be hoped that the diminished cost, by the impetus it will give to the cultivation of music, will again have the effect of creating fresh buyers in addition to those which already exist.

"The *second question* may be best answered by a consideration of the facts, that the music they have purchased could not have been published at a lower price during the limited demand occasioned by the then state of musical taste, and that they have been compensated by an earlier, a longer, and an exclusive enjoyment of it; he whose means and inclination enable him to indulge in green peas at a guinea the quart in *January*, does not complain because everyone can obtain the same luxury for a shilling the peck in *June*.

"I have thought it more just to make this large reduction at once, in anticipation, as it were, of the growing taste, than to make partial reductions, occurring several times: and the reduced price, marked in plain figures, is adjusted on an equitable scale.

"I have thus fully stated my reasons for making so extensive a change in price, in the hope of satisfying any objections which might arise in the minds of such musicsellers and professors as do not take into consideration that, by imparting to *the Million* the refinement of art, they are not only usefully and honourably employed, but are not so liable to be affected by fluctuations arising out of the caprices of fashion; but lest the object of affording the public increased facilities should be impeded by those who think this new arrangement injurious to them, I think it right here to state that my publications are

NEVER OUT OF PRINT,

and if one dealer will not supply them, another will; or the musical amateur will always find a supply by direct application to the *London Sacred Music Warehouses*, 69, Dean Street, Soho, and 24, Poultry.—January 1st, 1849."

The success of this further experiment was beyond expectation. The old plates were printed and reprinted to supply the demand, and every work upon which the reduction was made had the altered cost stamped in red letters. Thus a piece which formerly cost sixpence was marked "reduced price, threepence," and so on. As soon as new plates were required, the altered charge was retained until at length the "reduced price" became the standard charge.

In the months of March, April, and May, 1849, a new edition of Boyce's Collection of Cathedral Music in score was published by subscription in three volumes, at a guinea and a-half each volume to subscribers. The work was issued under the immediate sanction and patronage of Her Most Gracious Majesty Queen Victoria, to whom it was also (by permission) dedicated. Boyce's selection and arrangement were adhered to in their integrity, so that the new copies could be used with the old where they existed. It was largely taken up by amateurs and used in the several churches where choral service was employed. A few Cathedrals subscribed to the work, but the greater number of copies was bought by private people. The publication of Boyce's Cathedral Music was not due to the patronage of the Church, even in its original form.*

The reduced prices, which enabled purchasers to possess vocal parts and all sheet music at the rate of three-halfpence per page, were so far successful that they not only became the standard in the house of Novello, but they also served as the model charge for publications by other firms throughout England and the Continent. The public press com-

---

* Dr. Arnold, in the preface to the continuation which he published, says: "Many inaccuracies having crept into the books of the various choirs in and about this kingdom through the ignorance or inattention of transcribers, Dr. John Alcock, of Litchfield, published proposals for printing by subscription some of the services, in order to correct and preserve them from such injuries in future. Dr. Greene being now at the head of his profession, and finding himself, by the death of his uncle, Sergeant Greene, in a state of affluence, possessing (exclusive of his appointments) £700 per annum, he opposed Dr. Alcock's scheme, and publicly announced his intention of presenting to the Cathedrals, at his own expense, one correct copy, in score, of the works of the ancient masters celebrated for Church music. Dr. Alcock, therefore, relinquished his plan, and presented Dr. Greene with his MSS., the labour and research of many years. Dr. Greene dying, bequeathed the MSS. to his pupil, Dr. Boyce, who subsequently completed and published the work."

mended the venture, and the spirit of the enterprise was recognised on all sides. In a review of Novello's cheap oratorios which appeared in the *Morning Herald* of this date, among other statements are the following: "These works are issued at a price that literally places them within the reach of the million. The size (royal octavo) scarcely exceeds that of many operatic librettos, and hence the value of the publications as companions to the concert-room; while the exquisite beauty of the typography and the tasteful illumination of the binding give them a drawing-room character, which will also be duly prized and applauded. Although the type is small, it is wonderfully distinct, and in this respect is greatly superior to the printing by metal plates, with which modern ingenuity has made us familiar; but, above all, the oratorios emanate from the press under the control and supervision of Mr. Vincent Novello, whose name ensures the fidelity of the text, and the certainty that the responsibilities of editorship are vigilantly and critically discharged. The success of the enterprise has, we believe, been unbounded; and we have been informed that some 20,000 copies of 'The Messiah' alone have already been sold. To the works we have enumerated, Mr. Novello has added, in similarity of form and price, Mendelssohn's 'St. Paul,' and we observe that Handel's 'Israel in Egypt' is in course of periodical issue. We can but commend the series to the attention of those who have not yet met with them, for they more than justify the publisher's profession of cheapness, and in every respect warrant the admiration which has been so lavishly bestowed upon them."

Among other publications of this year was the Rev. Thomas Helmore's "Psalter Noted"; Mr. Joule's "Directorium Chori Anglicanum"; and, after a delay caused by the exaction of certain taxes on knowledge, the completion in two volumes of Novello's Cathedral Choir Book, with a dozen or so of sacred songs by various composers, including a new edition of Vincent Novello's famous "Infant's Prayer," which Madame Clara Novello, his daughter, was wont to sing with so much effect.

The "permanent enlargement of *The Musical Times* to sixteen pages," testifies to the recognition of the growing importance of that periodical.

In April, 1850, the prospectus of Novello's Part-song Book, edited by Edwin George Monk, Mus. Bac., Oxon., organist of St. Peter's College, Radley, was issued. The design of the originator and editor was to supply a collection of vocal music, attractive yet solid in character; which, while broad, bold, and interesting, shall still be pure and classical, and such as a scientific musician need not hesitate to place in the hands of a pupil. The words were to be selected as far as possible from the English poets, "but the editor will be compelled to have recourse, occasionally, to original sources, for songs adapted to the various Seasons, Sports, and Occupations of life—those being subjects which have but rarely received poetical treatment."

The proprietors appropriated £100 per annum to be expended in musical premiums, and a premium of eight guineas was offered monthly for the best part-song for four voices, composed and adapted to the stanzas given in the current number. It was published

Taxes on Musical Knowledge.

on the fifteenth of the month, price one shilling, each number containing three pieces. Among the contributors were the editor, G. A. Macfarren, J. Benedict, E. F. Rimbault, &c. The first prize was gained by W. C. Macfarren for his "Harvest Song," the second by Elizabeth Stirling for "All among the barley," which enjoyed an extraordinary run of popularity. While speaking of this work, it may be as well to state that one of the quoted trials in the question of copyright, Novello *v.* Sudlow, arose out of this publication. Through a misapprehension of the law upon the subject, some injustice was done to the firm by the multiplication of copies of works without the consent of the owner of the copyright. The Liverpool Philharmonic Society made a number of copies of Benedict's "Wreath," one of the pieces in the serial (Novello's Part-song Book), for the use of its chorus at a performance. The society, through its secretary, Mr. Sudlow, was adjudged to have infringed the rights of the owner.

In the month of April, 1850, Mr. Alfred Novello petitioned the House of Commons, through Mr. Milner Gibson, on the subject of the taxes on musical knowledge. He stated that "It has been found the most convenient mode to publish his popular series of cheap oratorios, in numbers containing sixteen pages of music, to be ready at an ascertained time, and to keep their sheets clean they are stitched in a coloured wrapper; but the fact of having a date on the wrapper subjects the catalogue of his publications to advertisement duty, although books published with a catalogue bound with them are not liable; and if for the better arrangement of the catalogue, dividing rules are used between the works enumerated, then separate duties are charged. Musical works so printed have not any temporary or periodical character in their contents beyond the date of which they are ready for sale. The advertisement duty thus acts as a heavy tax on these useful and popular works, and in the case of Novello's Cathedral Choir Book (containing a mere reprint of church services) the duty was one of the main causes which stopped the work, for the Stamp Office insisted on the duty being levied, after representation was made of its small sale."

"That your petitioner is also publisher of a small monthly sheet called *The Musical Times*, consisting of a piece of music, a brief chronicle of passing musical events, and musical advertisements; price three-halfpence, or stamped, twopence halfpenny. The stamped edition is for the facility of sending through the post; but in order to obtain that convenience he has been subjected to the Newspaper Act, which requires every proprietor not only to give security for the payment of the advertisement duty, but also to enter into recognizances to Her Majesty the Queen, by himself and others, to the amount of £1,200, that he shall not insert a libel in *The Musical Times*, an offence which the nature of the work renders scarcely possible, and for which offence there are remedies, should the offence be committed. There are also heavy penalties enacted for failure to deliver at the Stamp Office copies of all works called periodicals or newspapers. That the Excise duty on paper is directly a very heavy percentage upon cheap musical publications, by enhancing the cost of the works themselves; but it is also indirectly so, by increasing the cost of the catalogues necessary to make them known."

Here was a list of grievances which made the courage of the publisher in reducing the price of his works worthy of being classed among high patriotic efforts. The present generation knows nothing of these disabilities, for it is due to the efforts of Mr. Novello and his colleagues that all these vexatious imposts were ultimately removed. Further, it will be seen by a quotation of the final paragraph of his petition that he had courage and foresight in asking, single-handed, for the removal of harassing taxes, and suggesting a means which ultimately proved of the highest value to the revenue:—

"Your petitioner therefore prays that the Excise tax upon paper, the tax upon advertisements, and the stamp tax upon newspapers may be abolished, leaving the authorities to fix a small charge for the transmission of newspapers by post."

All these suggestions are now conceded, and cheap music is not the only advantage posterity enjoys through the efforts of Alfred Novello.

In May, 1850, the New York branch is referred to, and Novello's "Glee Hive" is announced for publication weekly: "A complete glee or madrigal each week, varying in price according to length, at the rate of one halfpenny a page." The first number was published on the 3rd of August and continued until three volumes were completed.

The publication of five of Handel's full scores, "printed from the original plates engraved by Mr.

Walsh,"* which were corrected by Mr. Handel himself, and published in his lifetime—namely, "The Messiah," "Judas Maccabæus," "Acis and Galatea," "Zadok the Priest," and the "Dettingen Te Deum," the plates of which are still in existence (1887)—with some favourite pieces, " sung with so much effect by the singers of the Royal Berlin Choir, at the National Concerts at Her Majesty's Theatre, Haymarket," complete the noteworthy works and deeds of the year.

In 1851, the year of the first great Exhibition, purchase was made of some 4,780 plates, which comprised all the important sacred works in the catalogue of C. Coventry, besides some 1,427 plates of the newly engraved and complete edition of Mozart's pianoforte works, edited by Cipriani Potter, Principal of the Royal Academy of Music. These were published in nine volumes, price £7 7s. (formerly £16 16s.), and in thirty fortnightly parts, price 4s. 6d. each. Thematic catalogues were also issued; these being the first of the kind published in this country.

Eight Anthems, by S. Webbe, for the use of country choirs; the completion of the volume of the Part-song Book; of the first volume of the "Glee Hive"; and of Mary Cowden-Clarke's "Girlhood of Shakespeare's Heroines," a series of fifteen tales in fifteen numbers; with a continuation of W. T. Best's arrangements from the scores of the works

---

* This statement is copied from the advertisements in *The Musical Times* of the period. Walsh only published the songs, his successors, Randall and Wright, finished the works by adding the choruses. This was done after the death of the composer. Handel himself never saw a complete printed edition of any one of his oratorios.

of the great masters, and a few lesser works, were sent forth.

In May, 1852, the new edition of Sir John Hawkins's "General History of the Science and Practice of Music" was announced, in monthly parts, price 3s. 6d. each, two of which were equal in contents to one of the original five volumes. The whole of the text was printed "in its integrity, without alteration, together with the illustrative woodcuts of instruments, &c. (for which more than 200 wood-cuts have been engraved); the whole of the musical examples in the various ancient and modern notations, and the fac-simile examples of old manuscripts." Something more than this was done. All the notes added by Sir John Hawkins to his private copy deposited in the British Museum were inserted in the new edition, which, by this means, was augmented in value. The extra volume of portraits, &c., was printed from the original engraved copper plates. This undertaking was duly recognised by the musical public, and in fact it stands as a monument of the spirit and enterprise of the publisher at a time when musical literature was outside the reach of students. By bringing it within the grasp of all, a lasting benefit was conferred, and the further progress of art was helped, by the publication of one of the most trustworthy works on Musical History which, as far as it goes, has ever been issued.

In August of the same year, Mr. Alfred Novello found it necessary to establish a branch of his business in New York, 389, Broadway, in consequence of the increased demand for his music in

America. He sent from England an assistant who had been seven years in his London establishment, who was "thoroughly acquainted with every detail of the catalogue." Hitherto the business had been transacted through the medium of agencies, but now direct communication with the London house was fully made.

As increased activity marked the conduct of the operations of the house, a further expansion of the principles which had guided its operations— namely, the encouragement of the love for musical art—was displayed in the publication of the first of a series of treatises, &c., called "The Library for the Diffusion of Musical Knowledge." This was a translation, from the German, of Marx's "Allgemeine Musiklehre" (General Musical Instruction), by George Macirone.

This library also included Cherubini's Treatise on Counterpoint, and Catel's Treatise on Harmony, translated by Mary Cowden-Clarke, Fetis's Treatise on Choir and Chorus Singing, translated by the Rev. T. Helmore, and Albrechtsberger's Thorough Bass, Harmony, and Composition, Mozart's Succinct Thorough Bass School, translated by Sabilla Novello, and, later, Crotch's Elements of Musical Composition, and Berlioz on Instrumentation, translated by Mrs. Cowden-Clarke, &c. It is not generally known that Berlioz added the chapter on Conducting for the English edition of the latter work, thereby imparting to it a special value, to the great advantage of British musicians.

A series of Cathedral Services, by Farrant, Childe, Creyghton, Kempton, Kelway, Tomkins, Church, and Rogers, edited by Sir Frederick Ouseley, together with a book of Services and Anthems of his own composition, mark the first appearance of his name in the catalogues of the firm. These works were eagerly welcomed by the various church choirs which were now springing up in various places, all testifying to the continuous spread of the love for music, and the ardent desire to dedicate it to the highest service.

Choral societies had also increased in numbers, and demands for more copious supplies of music for their use suggested "a new facility for Choral Societies with moderate means," in the publication of " Novello's Octavo Choruses " from the Oratorios and Masses, which on their being added to the monthly issue of classical works had met with such favour from the public and the press. The increased facilities for communication afforded by the railway accommodation had extended the business considerably. The artistic and commercial visits to distant towns which Mr. Alfred Novello had been wont to make were undertaken by others where necessary. The customers of the house knew that they could trust the wares, and the head of the house, finding it impossible to approach them personally, did so by an occasional address printed in *The Musical Times* as an advertisement. In his *Musical Circular*, at the end of the year 1853, he states that " as the winter advances, and the longer darkness of the evenings gives more time for indoor amusements before it is bed-time, music (which had been disregarded during summer) resumes her sway. Holiday-making at the sea-side, or by excursion trains, has come to an end, and the scattered members of practising vocal and orchestral societies re-organise their meetings with fresh appetite from the recess. The natural sequence is to ask what has Mr. Alfred Novello been providing for us?" Then he details the newly-published works. In this year Pierson's "Jerusalem," "The deliverance of Israel," and "Isaiah," by W. Jackson, of Masham, the Chevalier Neukomm's "Mount Sinai" and "David," and other works which have served their purpose, and are now rarely spoken of or remembered, were then popular. In another circular, issued a month or two later, in 1853, mention is made of "the great success of the series of cheap oratorios," and of their "imitation by those who, having neither courage to undertake the risk of experiments nor public spirit to venture on what may be a sacrifice, are not ashamed to copy anyone's ideas when there is a prospect of sharing a benefit."

These imitations were not published at a less cost, but at the same prices as Novello's, "an involuntary proof of the equity with which these cheap works were priced by the originator."

In 1854 the octavo score of the "Creation" was reduced to three shillings, and "The Messiah" and "Judas Maccabæus" to four shillings each.

The exertions made from time to time to obtain a diminution of the taxes on knowledge were crowned with a further measure of success in 1855. Mr. Alfred Novello was threatened with a Government prosecution by one official department because *The Musical Times* was said to be a *newspaper*, and therefore ought not to be printed except upon stamped paper. On the other hand, another official department was about to confiscate the paper and send it to the Dead Letter Office, unless it was folded in a particular manner, because it was said to be *not strictly a newspaper.* Even a Government is not insensible to ridicule, and the absurdity of the position formed a new argument. "These opposite dangers were boldly combated, and we are proud to think that our paper has had some share in fighting that good fight which has necessitated the bill at present before Parliament, by which the periodical press of this country will be emancipated from that red stain of bondage—the Compulsory Stamp. This is a second and large instalment of relief from the restrictions hitherto limiting the spread of intelligence and information; and, should the blessings of peace succeed at an early day to the horrors of the present war, we may hope that, ere the completion of the seventh volume, we may have to record the removal of the heavy Excise duty on paper, the last remaining tax on knowledge—a tax which still presents so formidable an hindrance to the many efforts now making to improve the character of low-priced literature."

The use of the Newspaper Stamp became optional in 1855, when the book post was instituted, and it was announced that *The Musical Times* would no more be printed upon stamped paper, "but a penny stamp would be affixed when it was sent by post." Music when sent in like manner could be forwarded at the rate of four ounces for a penny. The Advertisement and other duties now being removed, a large number of newspapers were started, some to remain to the present day, others to die in their infancy.

The interest in musical matters at this period (1855-7) was steadily increasing, the inadequate accommodation in the existing rooms set apart for musical purposes was felt, and the endeavour was made to meet the new demand. Concerts were given in the Crystal Palace at Sydenham, a building constructed out of the materials employed in the Great Exhibition of 1851. A large hall was built in the Surrey Gardens, then a place of general amusement. A small collection of wild animals, a "panorama" over a lake, constructed to serve as a medium for a pyrotechnic display, and a colossal concert hall capable of holding 10,000 persons were the standard attractions. Here Jullien and his band introduced the people to the Symphonies of Haydn, Mozart, Beethoven, Mendelssohn, and others. At the West End of London people were talking about the new St. James's Hall, to be built in the "space between the Regent's Quadrant and Piccadilly." A new concert hall, St. George's Hall, had been projected. Cheap Monday evening Concerts at St. Martin's Hall—area, threepence; galleries, sixpence; reserved seats, one shilling—were inaugurated, with Mr. Leigh Hunt as president. Large audiences had patronised the cheap Organ Recitals in Liverpool and elsewhere. Choral societies were formed and flourished throughout the country. People of gentle birth did not disdain to allow their names to appear as vocal or instrumental performers in various localities, and everything showed that a better feeling than formerly existed with regard to music and its value as a humanising influence.

The publications of the house of Novello, which had been greatly instrumental in bringing about this state of things, were increasing in number and usefulness. More commodious premises were engaged for the City branch of the business. "Novello's City depôt is removed to 35, Poultry, corner of Grocers' Hall Court," was announced in July, 1856.

Other publishers began to copy the publications of the firm, the octavo size in particular, and to advertise them as "same size as Novello's," and so forth. The importance of the house was duly recognised, and its position firmly established. The moral advantages of the pursuit of the principles upon which it had been founded had been productive of great effects throughout all the land, and, in fact, in every place where the English tongue was spoken. The vast number of choral societies, large and small, which existed had been made possible by means of the "cheap music"; and the more important matter—a general improvement in the social life of the people—had been brought about by the consistent and persistent efforts of Alfred Novello. He now probably felt that he could afford to relax his labours, and enjoy the ease he had earned by much hard work of various kinds during a period of twenty-seven years. He had a sturdy lieutenant in the person of Mr. Henry Littleton, who had worked with him strenuously and conscientiously for fifteen years, and had made himself master of every detail of the business in all its varied forms. To Mr. Littleton's care then he entrusted the management of his affairs, and went to reside in Italy, the land of his predilection and the home of his paternal ancestors.

In January, 1857, Mr. Alfred Novello requested that letters on private business should be addressed to him at "Maison Quaglia, au Port, Nice, Sardinia," and from that day forward the task of carrying out and extending the operations of the firm was in the hands of Mr. Littleton.

His accession to power was coincident with a remarkable event in the history of the firm—namely, the issue, at reduced prices, of Centenary Editions of Handel's most popular Oratorios and Cantatas, complete for one shilling and sixpence, or two shillings each, and portions of them at the cost of a few pence, in order to facilitate the universal celebration of the proposed centenary commemoration in 1859 of the great Handel's death. These publications were got ready in time for the preliminary Handel Festival in 1857.

The cheap editions of the oratorios given at the Handel Festivals were supplied from Dean Street, and the committee entrusted the preparation of the book containing the various pieces performed upon the "Selection day" to the originators of the famous Octavo Editions. These were followed by works of other composers—Haydn, Mozart, and Beethoven. The success was beyond expectation, and produced "the usual inferior imitations." Other publishers adopted the octavo form. Messrs. Longman, for example, issued a new edition of Moore's Irish Melodies, with symphonies and accompaniments by Sir John Stevenson, in the same size; Mr. William Chappell's "Popular Music of the Olden Time," printed by Novello, was published in numbers, in imperial octavo, nearly the same size, and other publishers of more or less importance bore witness to the utility of the invention, for so it was, by adopting it.

The Handel Festival.

The example of the house had been imitated in various ways; the influence it had exercised had been felt in all directions. The most striking outcome was exhibited in the experimental Handel Festival, which took place at the Crystal Palace in June, 1857. The thought of the commemoration originated in the mind of Robert Kanzow Bowley, Manager of the Crystal Palace, and one of the most important members of the Sacred Harmonic Society. There is no necessity to dwell upon the details of this stupendous achievement, the story has been often told. Suffice it to say that the experience gained by the Sacred Harmonic Society during its existence, then for a quarter of a century, enabled it to supply a most perfect organisation of the forces. The forces themselves, drawn from all parts of the country, had been chiefly nourished, if not actually raised, by the cheap publications of the house of Joseph Alfred Novello.

HENRY LITTLETON.

CHAPTER III.

1858—1867.

"Hath he provided this music?"
    Much ado about nothing, Act i., Sc. 2.

DURING the course of the year 1857, an experiment had been quietly tried with a result that was in every way satisfactory. The desire of the publisher was realised, and the prospect of further extending the love for art in one of its most valuable forms opened out brightly. This was to provide by degrees a series of compositions, by the best living writers, for the use of the service of the Church of England. The first work was an anthem, "O praise the Lord," written by John Goss, organist of St. Paul's Cathedral, in December, 1856, for the enthronement of the Bishop of London (the Right Rev. Dr. Jackson). It was intended to be sung in procession, and was available with or without accompaniment. The demand for this simple and effective composition was very great, and the composer was asked to write other anthems of like kind. This he agreed to do, and provided for the March number of *The Musical Times*, in time to be of use at Easter, one entitled "Christ our Passover," and another, "Behold I bring you good tidings," for Christmas. In response to the invitation of the practical head of the firm, Goss wrote many pieces well calculated to add dignity to the service of the Church. "The whole of the musical world then became alive to the fact that there was a great genius in its midst, a genius whom circumstances had kept silent until he had arrived at the age when most men cease to speak. From that time forward, until within a few years of his death, he enriched the stores of church music with works heard every day in one or other of our Cathedrals, which preach the truths of religion more forcibly than many sermons."* Dr. E. G. Monk, organist at Radley College, afterwards of York, and Dr. Ions of Newcastle, wrote two excellent Christmas carols, which were printed in the November number of *The Musical Times*, in time to be of use at the festive season. These last-named writers also produced two Easter carols, printed in 1858, and Mr. E. J. Hopkins composed his Easter anthem, "Why seek ye the living among the dead?" all being first printed in *The Musical Times*. In the pages of the same periodical no less than eight new anthems by G. J. Elvey, W. H. Monk, E. J. Hopkins, and J. Goss, besides other sacred and secular pieces by ancient and modern composers, appeared in due course during the year.

Until the appearance of these anthems, little else but large works and collections by English composers had been given to the world; nothing having been done to bring forward composers representing the present century. Since then thousands of Services and Anthems have been published, many at the small cost of three-halfpence each.

In April of the same year, Moore's Irish Melodies, with new symphonies and accompaniments for the pianoforte, by M. W. Balfe, himself an Irishman, were

---

* English Church Composers, by W. A. Barrett. Sampson Low and Co.

issued in one volume, two hundred and forty pages, price twenty-five shillings, containing seventy-three of the most popular of the melodies; also seventeen of them arranged as vocal duets, and a selection of fifty for four voices. The collection was also issued in twelve monthly parts, price two shillings each, and later in three octavo volumes, containing (1) the solos; (2) the duets; and (3) the quartets. This was a splendid work. It contained a special preface by J. W. Davison, recognising the ability Balfe had displayed in discharging his task. The purity of the melodies was respected, and the accompaniments were happily and genially fitted to the spirit of the songs, so that their characteristic qualities should not be sacrificed, as in Sir John Stevenson's arrangements, by extraneous ornamentation, ill suited to the simplicity of the ideas.

The printing and publication of Hymns Ancient and Modern was undertaken for the Rev. Sir H. Baker, the head of a society of some forty clergymen, who proposed to guarantee the expenses of production among them. Before the work was completed a few specimen pages of words and tunes were printed and sent to many of the clergy who were likely to favour the idea, to court their co-operation. An advertisement inserted in the *Guardian*, asking for help, brought replies from over two hundred clergymen, besides laymen. The specimen pages alluded to were issued in the spring of the year 1859, and the complete work at the beginning of 1860.

The success of the work was enormous. It was beautifully printed, the form was novel, and the people were ready for its reception. It is no exaggeration to say that many millions of copies of the various editions were sold within a few years.

It may not be out of place here to mention that *The Musical Times*, which, upon its first establishment, sold only a few hundred copies monthly, had now attained a circulation of 10,500. This was independent of the subsequent sale of the music contained in each number, and refers only to the first impression, containing the advertisements, articles on music, notices of concerts and of singing societies. These articles were eagerly read, the number of advertisements increased, testifying to the growing importance of the journal, and to its recognition as the chief organ of communication between all who were interested in music, whether as an art, a science, or a trade.

The chief musical event of the year 1859 was the great Handel Festival at the Crystal Palace in June, which of course gave rise to considerable activity in the house; for Alfred Novello was again entrusted by the Sacred Harmonic Society to print the musical copies necessary for the performers at the Commemoration, and by the directors of the Crystal Palace Company to provide the octavo hand-books for the use of the audience. He was also authorised to print the whole of the music for the Wednesday's selection, in the order of performance, which was published uniform with his editions of Handel's "Messiah" and "Israel in Egypt." A pocket edition of the former was published at one shilling and fourpence for this festival.

Inspired by the success of the festival, it was proposed, in certain musical circles, to establish a

Popular Concerts.

"Handel College" for the orphans of musicians. A plot of ground (the value of which was estimated at £5,000) was offered gratuitously, and Mr. Horace Jones likewise gratuitously consented to act as the architect.* The Vocal Association, of which Mr. Benedict was the chairman, undertook to superintend the business details of the scheme, and appeals were made to the public for funds. The institution was never established, and the project remains yet to be carried out.

More successful results attended the experiment of giving classical music at cheap prices at the Monday Popular Concerts, which were begun in February, 1859, under the direction of Mr. S. Arthur Chappell. After the first season they became one of the permanent musical institutions of London. Additional performances on Saturdays have brought the number of concerts already given to beyond a thousand.

About the same period the Crystal Palace Saturday Concerts, which were established in 1855, assumed the form which gained for them a very high reputation, not only in England, but on the Continent of Europe. This result was chiefly attained by the careful and enthusiastic action of the conductor, Mr. August Manns, and of the then secretary of the Crystal Palace, Mr. George Grove. Both of these enterprises are distinctly worth remembering in a sketch of the History of Cheap Music. Their educational value was greatly enhanced by the admirable

---

* A great portion of the details prepared for the College was used in the construction of the Guildhall School of Music a quarter of a century later.

analytical programmes provided, in the first case, by J. W. Davison, and, in the second, by Mr., now Sir, George Grove. The analytical programme, first used by John Ella in connection with the concerts of the Musical Union, has become an indispensable accompaniment to all concerts arranged upon an intellectual basis.

Among the publications of this year were the full scores of "The Messiah" and the "Creation," price forty-two shillings each, the first venture of the kind made by the house. These works, not only for themselves, but as indications of continued activity, were regarded with satisfaction by the few who could estimate the value of the new departure; the many hailed with greater delight the desire to extend the *répertoires* of church choirs by the issue of original compositions by living composers, which was not the only one of the operations which distinguished the firm during the year.

The festivals held in Glasgow, Bradford, and Gloucester, among the more important places in Great Britain at the time, were helped by the publications of the firm, and accounts received from the colonies show that music, actively practised in the "far off cities of the earth," was made easy and interesting by its varied editions. The New York branch was now carried on at 1, Clinton Hall, Astor Place, and the musical works were as highly valued in America and in the dependencies of the British Crown as at home. Some of the fiscal restrictions of the United States had been modified, while at home the agitation for the repeal of the last of the taxes on knowledge was kept up with undiminished vigour. Musical

The Village Band.

instruments of French manufacture were admitted to England free of duty, and, as a consequence, harmoniums, organines, and organ accordions made abroad became popular, and necessitated the production of musical compositions and arrangements suitable for their use. The old village band, the fiddles, hautboys, clarinets, bassoons, and bass viols had been sneeringly laughed out of favour, and the harmonium, being portable, and controllable by a single player, was preferred.

In 1860 Attwood's Cathedral Music, in vocal score, with accompaniment for the organ, by his godson, Thomas Attwood Walmisley, in one volume (241 pages), with the Cathedral music (297 pages) of Walmisley himself, arranged by his father, Thomas Forbes Walmisley, were added to the publications of the house. Each work cost one guinea and a half, but there were separate vocal parts at three-half-pence a page. Some organ and vocal music by Mr. W. T. Best were also announced, and the chorus parts of the operas "Der Freyschütz," "Oberon," "Idomeneo," and "La Gazza ladra" were offered at the usual cheap rate.

The Rifle Volunteer movement had called many brass bands into existence, and the low rates at which instruments of French make could be obtained diverted the cultivation of music into other channels than those which were occupied by the singing societies. These flourished as vigorously as ever, while the programmes which were performed publicly gave evidence of higher ambition in the selections than heretofore. Domestic music was also assiduously cultivated, and it is not a little singular that the last

G

publication to which Vincent Novello's name was attached was called "Home music; or, Congregational and Choristers' Psalm and Hymn Book, containing selections from Handel, Haydn, Mozart, Beethoven, Winter, Paisiello, Hummel, Herold, Webbe, and Novello." It was intended to supply the demand made in consequence of the greater attention paid to music in the home circle. On the 9th of August in the following year the great pioneer of cheap music breathed his last at Nice in his eightieth year.* "By descent an Italian, the larger part of his life and his professional career were passed in London, where his sound musical knowledge, and his command over the organ (then not common in England) enabled him to do valuable service to his art. Especially was this rendered in the naturalisation of sacred music of the great Italian and German writers belonging to the Roman Catholic Church. The Masses of Mozart, Haydn, Hummel, and many writers less known—still meriting to be known—owe the largest share of their introduction in a complete form to Mr. Novello's editorship, and to their performance in the Portuguese Chapel, to which he was during many years attached. He was also an influential member of the Council of the Philharmonic Society (of which he was one of the founders in 1813), in the days when to belong to the same was a European distinction. He composed much, but what he produced was rather the work of an honest and temperate musician, perfectly trained, than the product of genius. That he was esteemed as a man

---

* He was born in London on September 6th, 1781. His father was an Italian, his mother an Englishwoman.

—that his society was cultivated beyond the verge of his own profession—will be seen (to name but one instance) in the letters of Elia. He had a numerous family, and to their distinction in his own art, and in the world of letters, it would be superfluous to advert. No common respect is implied in our farewell to one of the most sterling musicians of the old school whom this country has possessed as a resident." This was the tribute to his memory offered by a distinguished writer in the *Athenæum*. His monument, raised by himself and his children, exists in the operations and influence of the house which still bears his name.

In the month of November, 1861, the "style and title" of the firm was changed to " Novello and Co." In announcing this change it was stated—" J. Alfred Novello has the pleasure to inform the public, his friends, and patrons that from this date he has admitted Mr. Henry Littleton (for many years his assistant) to a partnership in his musicselling and printing establishments. The business, which has so long enjoyed the advantage of Mr. Henry Littleton's services, will be carried on under the denomination of Novello & Co., with the old anxiety to supply the best music at the most moderate prices. It will be the study of the new firm to equal and to exceed (if possible) the attention and promptitude with which they have at all times endeavoured to execute the orders of their musical patrons."

The issue of a new serial work, to be continued as occasion required, called "Novello's Octavo Edition of Church Services," was one of the first acts of the new firm. The interest in choral music had taken a new departure, and the several church choirs were forming themselves into Diocesan associations.* These were trained by local teachers, guided in their methods by a travelling inspector, who visited the various choirs in his district, and gave special instruction and direction concerning the performance of the works selected for the year, so that some degree of uniformity of idea might be attained when the whole of the choirs met in their local Cathedral. The books for these "festivals," as they were called, were printed by the new firm. They contained the versicles and responses, the chants for the psalms, and the hymns to be sung on the occasion. The Anthem, when one was appointed to be sung, was naturally selected and furnished from the vast stores in the possession of the firm of Novello & Co.

The Handel Festival at the Crystal Palace, now established as a triennial gathering, took place in 1862, and in the same year the International Exhibition was held at Kensington. In the autumn Novello and Co., not wanting in the enterprise which distinguished these important institutions, offered to the musical world a new pocket edition of Haydn's "Creation," complete with pianoforte or organ accompaniment, for one shilling; Handel's "Israel" at the same price, and an edition of Locke's "Macbeth" music, edited by C. D. Collet, in vocal score, with pianoforte accompaniment,

* In 1851 the Choir Benevolent Fund, a society for the benefit of lay clerks and organists in Cathedrals, was established, and by its festival services—given once, sometimes twice, in a year, with a large body of voices, in the various metropolitan and provincial Cathedrals—may be said to have initiated those diocesan choral gatherings which have now become so popular throughout the kingdom.

Organ Music.

octavo size, price sixpence. Mendelssohn's "Six Grand Sonatas" for the organ, Op. 65, complete in one volume, were, with two volumes of Hiles's Short Voluntaries, selected from various composers, placed at the command of the numerous organ and harmonium players then spread over the country. An edition of Sir Henry Bishop's Glees and Choruses, commenced in December with twenty-one pieces, to be continued, closed the list of the year, and testified to the unabated energy with which the firm was working.

Mr. Best's six Concert Pieces for the Organ, his fine setting of the "Benedicite, omnia Opera," with a free organ part ; Mr. Benedict's new Part-songs, many of the most popular of Bishop's Glees, and the second edition of the Rev. J. Powell Metcalfe's "School Round Book" were among the publications of the beginning of the year 1863. Mendelssohn's four books of Four-part songs for singing in the open air, with English words by Sabilla Novello, were now reduced in price to one shilling each book. The price of this work was lowered still further three years later—the price of the whole four books being only eightpence. The "Glee Hive," three volumes, was also reduced to five shillings each volume, the separate numbers being made proportionately cheaper. Other works were also lessened in price, and new works were constantly added to the catalogue. The Bristol Tune Book ; further editions of Hymns Ancient and Modern ; Pearsall's Twenty-four Choral Songs and Madrigals ; Novello's Collection of Anthems for Parish Choirs, called into existence by the spread of diocesan associations, now contained works by Attwood, Barnby, Sterndale Bennett, Jules Benedict, W. T. Best, Langdon Colborne, Dr. Elvey, Dr. Gauntlett, John Goss, E. J. Hopkins, J. L. Hopkins, Henry Leslie, G. A. Macfarren, R. Mann, Dr. Monk, W. H. Monk, Sir Frederick Ouseley, V. Novello, H. Smart, G. Townshend Smith, Dr. Spark, Dr. Steggall, Dr. R. P. Stewart, A. Sullivan, and Dr. Walmisley; the "Life and Labours of Vincent Novello," by his daughter, Mary Cowden-Clarke, reprinted from *The Musical Times*, and issued in book-form; Goss's famous Harvest Anthem, "Fear not, O land"; Monk and Ouseley's Psalter; six Four-part Songs by Henry Smart; Westbrook's Voluntaries for the Organ; and twelve Choral Songs by G. A. Macfarren are among the more important publications of the year.

In the month of August a memorial window, executed by Lavers and Barraud, was placed near to the seat so often occupied by Vincent Novello, in Westminster Abbey. Thus an honourable testimony to the labours of one who had done so much for the promotion of a love for sacred music among his countrymen was raised among the tombs of the poets, the artists, and others who had in their life-time worked for the elevation of mankind.

The year 1864 was comparatively uneventful in the cause of musical art. Societies were continued rather than increased, but the nature of their operations assumed a greater refinement of character. This is shown in the extension of the number of part-songs, all of which required a special amount of care and expression for their due execution. The pattern of careful singing in this style of work had been set by

Mr. Henry Leslie's Choir, an institution which had been originally framed and organised by Mr. Joseph Heming in 1855. The choir not only formed the model for the proper performance of known pieces, but awakened a desire among amateurs and choirs of less importance than themselves to attain to more careful execution; they also spurred our native composers to exertions to supply an ever increasing demand for that form of composition which was the legitimate successor of the glee and the madrigal. A writer in *The Musical Times* thus speaks of the matter: "The part-song which, without wishing to disturb the madrigal as a pure specimen of a certain time and school, seems more in accordance with our present musical requirements, is, we think, destined to supersede that quaint form of composition so successfully carried out in this country, at a time when the art was still struggling for life and freedom."

The growing demands made by those who favoured the Tonic Sol-fa method of notation were met by the publication of editions of the Bristol Tune Book, Hymns Ancient and Modern, &c., in that method; otherwise the year showed no great advances as compared with former years. By degrees a vast number of pieces, including many cantatas, oratorios, &c., translated by Mr. W. G. McNaught, were added to the list of publications, until, in 1887, the total amounted to upwards of six hundred works in this notation. The house of Novello & Co. was more prosperous than ever, and perhaps busier; but all its exertions were devoted to solidifying rather than extending its operations. Mr. Henry C. Lunn, who became editor in 1863, in his review of the season in *The Musical Times*, shows pretty clearly the state of things outside when he says: — "In the season just past we see more strongly than ever the growing tendency to place the art in as few hands as possible. At the Royal English Opera (now definitely closed) the effort to produce a musical work nightly with the same artists was painful in the extreme; and even at Her Majesty's Theatre, where things should be better managed, we have an example of one vocalist (Mdlle. Titiens) supporting almost alone an arduous season, and enlisting sympathy where her splendid talents should command unmixed admiration. In the concert room, classical pianoforte music seems to be represented to the public on the principle of those barometers where the lady and gentleman come out alternately, so that you may be pretty sure of a tolerably fair division of labour between them; but although we may agree that in all cases this duty is efficiently performed, even those who most admit their accuracy may occasionally long for variety. Against this system, as a mere matter of art, we should feel impelled to enter our protest; but when we see that, apart from this, many professors of first-rate powers are content to remain silent for want of an audience, we feel an additional desire to record our opinion that as the art widens there should be more room for artists, and that a fair and impartial hearing should alone decide by whom this additional room should be occupied."

At the beginning of the year 1865 Novello's Standard Glee Book, being a collection of the most favourite glees by English composers, was published in thirty numbers at one penny each. Each number

Advance of Sacred Music.

contained two glees, therefore the charge was at the rate of one halfpenny a glee, a price which served to spread a greater knowledge of these masterworks of native art. The publication by the firm of some of the early works of John Stainer, Arthur Sullivan,* C. Hubert H. Parry, George M. Garrett, Gerard F. Cobb, J. Barnby, Hamilton Clarke, and other now well-known writers; new Services and Anthems by John Goss; new Organ Arrangements and Compositions by Nixon, Best, Cooper, Oakeley, &c., also distinguish the events of the year.

"Sacred music," says *The Musical Times* in September, "is advancing throughout England with rapid strides, and there can be little doubt that the constant establishment of choral societies must eventually have a most beneficial effect upon the performance of the services in our churches. Much discussion has arisen, and is daily arising, upon the precise manner in which music is to be employed in our religious worship; but meantime it behoves us all to remember that, however small may be the portion of our service in which it is used, it should be given with all due attention and earnestness. Music is a gift which we should be additionally careful not to abuse when we approach our Divine Giver in the humble spirit of thankfulness and devotion."

The Handel Festival given at the Crystal Palace this year proved to be a great success, musically and financially. The possibility of making it even more

---

* Sullivan's first work was a sacred song, "O Israel," on the title-page of which he is described as chorister of the Chapel Royal; it was published in February, 1855, when he had not attained his thirteenth year.

profitable, alike to the cause of music as to the promoters of the scheme, was suggested by the formation of a London contingent of choralists. They were to meet from time to time as ordinary choral societies for the practice of the choruses of Handel, and other works, and by study and proper direction were to strive to attain even greater perfection than that already achieved on former occasions. The advantage of a London contingent, constantly subjected to one direction and control, would, it was hoped, secure greater precision and uniformity of attack than could be possibly obtained by the one rehearsal which it was only possible to get when the various members of the chorus came from a distance. Twenty or even ten years before, such a scheme would have been impossible of execution; but the greater acquaintance with music obtained through the choral societies and the church choirs made it easy of accomplishment now. The applications to join from those who were qualified to pass the test were greatly in excess of the demand. This is the strongest proof of the universal spread of music that could be produced. In 1837 there were so few chorus singers in London that the Sacred Harmonic Society was compelled to look for a supply from Yorkshire and Lancashire, as a nucleus for their performances. These singers, having no other occupation, were supported by the society and its friends in the intervals of time between the engagements of the society and those which could be obtained elsewhere for them. In 1865 there were five thousand chorus singers, duly qualified and willing to give their services gratuitously for the sake of art.

Men usually congratulate themselves upon the attainment of small things. Those who achieve great things can afford to be silent. If it were seemly to boast, the house of Novello and Co. might indulge with pride and a just amount of warranty. The firm had had no actual hand in the formation of this contingent, yet it had been instrumental in preparing the way for it, and was ready to provide the vital nourishment which should keep it alive and vigorous. There would have been, therefore, a reasonable ground for expressions of joy on the part of those who had initiated the work and had seen it flourish and abound.

Among the final publications of the year may be mentioned George Cooper's "Organist's Assistant: a series of movements selected and arranged from the works of classical authors, and dedicated to the organists of the United Kingdom," and "The Organist's Manual"—recently acquired by the firm —an Elementary Method for the Organ or Harmonium, by the Chevalier Sigismond Neukomm; a number of valuable additions to the list of Anthems by Modern Composers; a Selection from the Works of Palestrina, in vocal score, arranged by J. M. Capes and Vincent Novello; and John Pratt's Collection of Anthems, arranged from various Italian, German, Spanish, and other composers, set to English words, selected from the Bible and Prayer Book. This last-named compilation had been in great use in that period when there was a dearth of native composers for the Church. Its re-appearance at a time when the firm had formed the taste of the public for new works by English composers showed how old and new ideas still ran side by side, and commanded a considerable measure of attention.

In 1866 Mr. Henry Littleton, who had been in the business since 1841, and had seen it through its infant days, when there was scarcely enough work to employ more than a few hands all through the year, and by his assiduity and patient attention had helped to build it up stone by stone, became its sole proprietor. Alfred Novello had long since ceased to take an active personal part in the conduct of the affairs of the firm. He now completely severed his connection with it. He was certain that the principles on which the house was founded fifty-five years before would, in the hands of his worthy successor, be faithfully maintained and perseveringly pursued. Outside the business the matters which had engaged his attention were all satisfactorily settled, and there was nothing left which was either oppressive or hindering to the constant and steady march of intellect. The taxes on knowledge, defined as such by the society of which Alfred Novello was, for many years, the treasurer, no longer existed. The first, the Advertisement Duty, had been repealed in 1853 ; the second, the Compulsory Stamp on Newspapers, in 1855 ; and the last impost, the Duty on Paper, in 1861. For these services Alfred Novello might have had a knighthood, had he not declined the honour when it was suggested by his friend and colleague in this work, Mr. Milner Gibson. All was now free and unfettered, and the course of education could be traversed without fear of vexatious stumbling-blocks placed in the way by the powers whose duty it should have been to see that the road was clear.

It is inconsistent with the enlightenment of modern times to find that men were so far enamoured with the legal restrictions which belonged to a past age that they employed every endeavour to retain them in the present.

At this time there was a growing wish to encourage morning performances and concerts. The chief place for these entertainments was the Hanover Square Rooms. Speaking of the matter, *The Musical Times* of December, 1865, says, "It appears that some legal archæologists have lately dug up a fossil Act of Parliament, which, instead of duly repealing it as a curiosity which might have been serviceable in its day, they have actually endeavoured to put into active use. The license applied for by the proprietor of the Hanover Square Rooms was lately almost refused because it seems that the letter of the law is that 'in no licensed house, room, or garden shall musical performances take place before five o'clock in the afternoon.' It was scarcely wise to rouse the absurd Act, after a peaceful slumber of so many years, considering that every thinking person in the present day looks upon the whole licensing system as a monstrous farce. No doubt, on the meeting of Parliament, this law will be repealed ; for there can be no discussion on the merits of an enactment which virtually declares that a sonata of Beethoven's at the Hanover Square Rooms at three o'clock has a more injurious tendency than 'Slap-bang' at the music halls at midnight."

These words produced the desired effect, and morning concerts were no longer prohibited, nor the license of the "house, room, or garden" imperilled by the performances. *The Musical Times*, which, at first, only aimed at the encouragement of singing in classes, had in the course of the twenty-two years of its existence become a recognised power in the musical world. Reports of musical events in London were written with judgment and increased in number; the brief summary of country news included also occasional notices of musical affairs in the colonies; so that, as it was not then expedient to increase the size of the paper, it became necessary to employ a smaller type to get in all the notices of interest; the advertisements increased in number and importance, and demonstrated the fact that the value of the paper was admitted by the trade, as well as by musicians, and, in short, it became the "abstract and brief chronicle of our time," a record of things passing and to come.

One of the earliest publications given to the world after Mr. Littleton's accession to the sole power was Novello's Parish Choir Book, published under the patronage of the members of the Ely Diocesan Church Music Society, who, "finding that one of the principal *desiderata* among parish choirs was an arrangement, or rather several arrangements, of the *Te Deum laudamus*, adapted especially for country churches, determined to endeavour to supply the want. Accordingly they put themselves in communication with some of the most eminent church music composers, and also with Messrs. Novello & Co. Several composers entered into their views, and Messrs. Novello & Co. expressed themselves as being willing to co-operate heartily in the work." The first fruits of this effort appeared in the compositions supplied by such eminent composers as Dr. Armes, G. B. Allen, Dr. Arnold, W. T. Best, J. Barnby, J. B. Calkin, Hamilton Clarke, G. M. Garrett, J. L. Hopkins, G. A. and Walter Macfarren, and Sir Frederick Ouseley.

A second volume of Special Anthems for certain seasons, by various living composers, edited by the last named, was published by subscription. This completed the provision of Anthems for special seasons and occasions which had been begun in a former work.

Of equal importance in another degree, and significant of entry into wider fields of usefulness, was the issue of Charles Gounod's St. Cecilia "Messe Solennelle," with English and Latin words; and the "Seven words of our Saviour on the Cross," also with English and Latin words. This served to bring before the British public in the most forcible way the genius of Charles Gounod as a representative modern musician; and together with the first of a series of Original Compositions for the Organ, by J. Lemmens, Léfèbure-Wély, Adolph Hesse, Ouseley, W. T. Best, Henry Smart, and others, indicated the new roads which the firm was opening.

A series of fifty-two Introits or Short Anthems, for holy-days and seasons of the English church, composed by G. A. Macfarren, and a small collection of Chants for the "Benedicite," indicated a desire to provide for the growing needs of the church service. The substitution of the "Benedicite, omnia Opera," in the place of the "Te Deum," had only been made in a few places; but they were representative, and the examples they furnished were likely to find many followers. Ten years later the custom was almost general.

At the beginning of the year 1867, the last in the third decade of the reign of Her Majesty, Mr. Joseph Barnby, who had been for several years their musical adviser, was requested by the firm to organise a choir for the practice of sacred and secular music, "with the view of presenting at public performances the best specimens of choral compositions, executed in the most finished style." The announcement of this intention was hailed with satisfaction by the musical world, and among the comments on the scheme the following may be quoted as most pertinent:—"Numerous as are the choirs in the metropolis for the interpretation of the great works of the classical composers, requiring large choral and orchestral resources, it is obvious that choirs especially trained for the due rendering of delicate part-music are extremely scarce, and, indeed, instead of its being true (as we have seen it stated) that choral societies are waiting for compositions to sing, we believe that some of the choicest of those works, especially those by accredited modern composers, are waiting for choirs to sing them. With the view, therefore, not of rivalling, but of healthily aiding the efforts of those choral societies which have already done so much for the cultivation of a love for part-music, this new choir has been formed. One of the features at the public concerts will, we understand, be the performance of those truly English compositions, glees, by the best glee-singers of the day, so that they may be heard as the composers wrote them, with one voice to each part. To us it has always appeared that the delicacy of these compositions is utterly destroyed when sung by a choir, however carefully trained in the observance of the

Removal to Berners Street.

minutest efforts of light and shade ; as well, indeed, might a string quartet be multiplied in the parts, until instead of a real quartet it assumes the character of a semi-orchestral work. One public performance of this new choir is announced to be given during the present season — a regular series of concerts being reserved for next year. We have little doubt that all persons desirous of increasing the spread of choral part-music will wish the utmost success to this society, especially as it will be conducted by a musician whose excellent training of the choir at the church of which he is organist has already proved his fitness for the task." These concerts were most successful in their artistic aims, and through their agency many young musicians, who afterwards became eminent, were introduced to the public.

The year 1867 marks another important epoch in the history of the house, inasmuch as the business of Ewer & Co. was acquired, and with it all the existing copyrights of Mendelssohn's compositions, such as "Elijah," "Athalie," "Walpurgis Night," "Hear my Prayer"—written for Mrs. Bartholomew's Concerts at Crosby Hall—with a number of standard works by other composers, besides the large and valuable circulating library of music which had already been extensively patronised. Increased accommodation was required, and the publishing and library businesses were removed in December to No. 1, Berners Street, an extensive range of premises, where it was hoped every section of the operations of the firm might find ample accommodation. This expectation was defeated, for the business increased to such an extent that there was scarcely enough accommodation for the two branches of music-publishing and music-lending. The printing business was at first carried on at Berners Street, but was afterwards removed back to the old publishing house, No. 69, Dean Street, to which was added, later on, No. 70, where some of the old engraved plates, bought at the sale of the effects of the firm of Coventry & Hollier, reposed once more near the shelves where they originally lay.

The removal to larger premises was not without attendant testimony, voluntarily acknowledged, to the importance of the firm. In 1867 Novello, Ewer & Co., with one exception, represented music in Berners Street. By degrees others came, until afterwards no less than nineteen houses connected with the music trade were established round about the warehouse of the pioneers of Cheap Music.

CHAPTER IV.

1868—1877.

" Whose music to my thinking pleased."
Henry IV., Part 2, Act v., Sc. 5.

ALTHOUGH a very large number of important publications were constantly being issued, perhaps the most remarkable work done during this decade consisted of the series of concerts given under the direction of the firm. The best music could be purchased at an exceedingly small charge, it was now necessary to prove that the same music could be heard at a similarly low rate of expense. Cheap concerts were shown to be as possible as cheap music. The house carried the idea to a practical issue, and made the first serious attempt to give a series of performances of great vocal and orchestral works, to which the public were admitted for one shilling. New works, and old masterpieces which had been neglected, were performed in the best manner at the lowest cost to the public. The seed was thus sown which has since developed into the great interest now taken in all new works.

The concerts alluded to in the last chapter seemed to be required to satisfy the public wishes. A valuable amount of good work was done by Henry Leslie and his choir in spreading a knowledge of partsinging, but there was room for other institutions which should keep this one point more conspicuously in view.

The firm, having, as before stated, appointed Mr.

Joseph Barnby their conductor, and having given two preliminary concerts in 1867, now announced a second season of four concerts, the first of which took place on the 29th of January, 1868. Mendelssohn's music formed the whole of the programme. "Athalie," with the illustrative verses recited by Mr. Henry Marston; The Reformation Symphony, second time in England; the "Trumpet" Overture, then recently published, and other items, which made a most attractive and successful concert and established the reputation of the choir. New works by Gounod and Mendelssohn and others were heard at these concerts; glees, madrigals, and motetts were given with a care and attention not always attained in public. Mr. Barnby's choir, by the introduction of new part-songs, &c., gave an impetus to this form of artistic work, which was a great gain both to musicians and the public. The one body was induced to supply new vocal works, and the other gladly received them, and proved how anxiously they had been waited for by studying them, taking them to heart, and firmly establishing their popularity. This object being gained, attention was turned to the domain of oratorio, then only occupied by the Sacred Harmonic Society. The society had already shown little inclination to undertake the production of new works until it was proved that such novelties were attractive and remunerative. The success achieved by Mr. Barnby's Choir led, in the following year, to the formation of the Oratorio Concerts. The first performance under the revised arrangement was given on February 5th, 1869. Handel's "Jephtha," revived for this occasion, with additional accompaniments by Arthur Sullivan, was the work selected for the opening concert. These concerts served to introduce the French, or rather Continental, pitch (*le diapason normal*) for the first time in England. "In the interest of vocalists, therefore, as well as in the interests of true art, it is desirable that the French pitch should be adopted in this country forthwith, and this important change will, as before stated, be inaugurated at these Oratorio Concerts." The controversy on Pitch was raised in consequence of certain criticisms in the daily newspapers *àpropos* of the first appearance of Miss Minnie Hauk in "La Sonnambula," at Covent Garden, in November, 1868. Mr. Sims Reeves had declined to sing for the Sacred Harmonic Society, in consequence of the high pitch asserted to have been employed, and the Oratorio Concerts received his best support and artistic help. An orchestra, composed of the best players procurable, added to the voices, which were selected "to gain effect by well-balanced power," afforded greater scope for work than could be attained on the plan of the original formation of the choir, and many important advantages were thereby gained by the establishment of this new venture. The house of Novello now made the endeavour to effect the further advance of art by giving concerts at which the best music received the best possible interpretation under favourable conditions. By these means the guiding principle, which had been carried to a successful issue in the way of publishing, was now being pursued by way of practical performances.

The press admitted the success of the experiment,

and it was hoped that "the *diapason normal* would gradually, but surely, become the recognised pitch of England." The process is probably still working, for the pitch has suffered little general change, despite the many leaders in the newspapers, the pamphlets, letters, and controversial correspondence. Madame Nilsson, Mr. Sims Reeves, Mr. John Hullah, Dr. W. H. Stone, and other influential musicians and amateurs expressed their views in various ways, but no permanently satisfactory result was achieved. The old proverb "Mus in pice," the mouse in a pitch barrel, applied to a man who wasted his time and temper in useless disquisitions and enquiries, seemed to be applicable to the present case.

During the second season, 1869-70, there were nine concerts. Beethoven's Mass in D was given as written, and not with the inverted passages for the voices used elsewhere. The sensation created by the work was most extraordinary. At the conclusion of the "Credo," although there was no interval, the audience grew so excited that many left their seats to confer with their friends in different parts of the room. The Choral Fantasia preceded the Mass. Bach's Passion-Music (according to St. Matthew), the Choral Symphony, Haydn's "Seasons," and other works formed the programmes of the season. The third season of the Oratorio Concerts began on February 15, 1871; the works presented were Bach's "Passion-Music" once more, Benedict's "St. Peter," Hiller's "Nala and Damayanti," the Mass in D and the Choral Symphony of Beethoven, &c., six concerts in all. Benedict's "St. Peter" had been

Royal Albert Hall Choral Society. 107

also given in the previous December as an extra concert.

There were ten concerts in the fourth season of 1871-2. These were given in Exeter Hall, on account of the better accommodation for the choir, now increased to 500 voices. Bach's "Passion-Music" was again one of the chief attractions, with Handel's "Jephtha," Mendelssohn's "Elijah," and other important works. Herr Stockhausen sang the part of *Elijah* for the first time in England during this season, and made a vivid impression on the minds of all who heard him.

The publication of Bach's "Passion-Music" according to St. Matthew, in the cheap octavo form, and its production at the Oratorio Concerts, led to the performance in Westminster Abbey, on Maundy Thursday, April 6, 1871, under the direction of Mr. Barnby. The effect of the sublime music, given in a sacred building for the first time in England, was inexpressibly beautiful; and this highly interesting event was the precursor and, without doubt, chief cause of the large number of musical services (with orchestra) which have since taken place in the Churches and Cathedrals all over the kingdom.

The Royal Albert Hall Choral Society was formed in 1871, with the Hon. Seymour J. G. Egerton, now Earl of Wilton, as superintendent of music. Mr. Charles Gounod, then residing in England, was appointed the first conductor.

Later, when Gounod resigned the conductorship, Mr. Barnby was appointed in his place, and the firm was asked to take the general direction of the society's work. The chorus was formed by an amalgamation of the Choral Society with the choir of the Oratorio Concerts. For the first season of six Subscription Concerts (1872-3), the principal works were "Belshazzar," "Passion-Music," "Israel in Egypt." The "Passion-Music," besides being included in these concerts, was also given in the Royal Albert Hall four times in Holy-week, on Monday, Tuesday, Wednesday, and Thursday, "The Messiah" being performed on Saturday. A peculiar feature in the presentation of the work was the fact of the audience accepting the invitation to rise and join in the chorals, the effect of which was to raise the performance above the level of a concert, and to elevate it to the position of a religious ceremony. As a result of the successful management of these performances the firm was invited by the Commissioners, who had seen the desirability of placing "music on view like the sister arts," to undertake the conduct of a series of concerts in 1873, when the London International Exhibition was held at Kensington. In obedience to this request daily concerts were given in the Royal Albert Hall, under the direction of Mr. Barnby, assisted occasionally by Herr Carl Deichmann. These concerts were attended by numbers who appreciated the opportunity of hearing an hour's music, consisting of an overture, a symphony, a march or concerto, with occasional vocal pieces, performed in the most finished style by competent artists. Visitors to the Exhibition were admitted free; a small fee for reserved seats only was charged, and the price of a programme, containing analytical and historical notes by Joseph Bennett, was threepence.

Among the features which distinguished them may be mentioned the production of music unknown or unfamiliar in England; the works of acknowledged great masters; and with a special view to the encouragement of musical composition in this country, prominence was given to the works of English composers; and advantage was taken to bring young artists and their works prominently before the public at these performances. These concerts commenced on Easter Monday, April 14, and were continued daily without intermission until the close of the Exhibition, October 31, upwards of two hundred performances having been given.

The second series of the Royal Albert Hall Oratorio Concerts, eleven in number, was begun on October 30, 1873. The most important works then performed included Bach's "Passion - Music" and "Christmas Oratorio," Handel's "Theodora," and Sullivan's "Light of the World," given for the first time in London. Oratorio was again given on every evening in Holy-week, March 30 to April 4, 1874, the "Passion-Music" being performed three times. In the same week it was given at St. Paul's Cathedral on March 31, and at Westminster Abbey in the afternoon of April 1.

The idea was now conceived of projecting perhaps the most important series of concerts ever given, with the highest artistic aims: every night concerts in the Royal Albert Hall.

On the 7th November, 1874, this series was commenced: Monday was the Ballad night, Tuesday the English night, Wednesday the Classical night, Thursday the Oratorio night, Friday the Wagner night, and Saturday the Popular night. Messrs. Dannreuther, Randegger, J. F. Barnett, W. H. Thomas, and Joseph Barnby divided the duty of conducting these concerts, which were continued through many weeks with success. Two choirs had to be organised for this work—a large one for the oratorios and a smaller one for the singing of part-songs, &c.

Nothing of the kind had ever been attempted before in any country in the world. The boldness of the idea was only equalled by the liberality with which the scheme was carried out. The immense amount of labour involved proved that the firm had higher considerations than those included in a mere commercial transaction. The programmes show an extraordinary degree of skill in arrangement and of cosmopolitan aim which is perfectly monumental.

The direct encouragement given to English composers was not the least remarkable feature of both series of these remarkable undertakings. Wagner's music, which was then comparatively new to England, was given on the Friday evenings as a special feature. The whole undertaking was in advance of the times, and the difficulty of access to the Albert Hall rendered it impossible to continue the scheme in its original form beyond seven weeks. The concerts were then given twice a week until May, 1875. These included the now well established Holy-week performances, from March 22 to 27. Bach's "Passion-Music" was again given three times, and in the month of May was followed by the production of Verdi's "Requiem." Verdi came to England in order to conduct the performances of his work, his visit being one of the most noteworthy events of the year 1875. The firm was requested by the owners of the copyright to undertake the entire direction ; and the choir was rehearsed by Mr. Barnby. The soloists were Madame Stolz, Mdlle. Waldmann, Signor Masini, and Signor Medini. Four performances were given, and an invitation rehearsal at the Royal Albert Hall, which was attended by numbers of distinguished personages in art, science, music, and literature. This was the last important work in connection with the Royal Albert Hall which was under the direct management of the firm, and formed a worthy conclusion to the great efforts in the cause of music which had been made since the work had been taken in hand by Messrs. Novello, in 1872. Very much had been done towards popularising the great building, and the Council was now enabled to form a committee to carry on oratorio performances, which continue to flourish to the present time. Messrs. Novello, Ewer & Co. then relinquished concert-giving until the time came for the present series of Oratorio Concerts referred to in the next chapter.

On November 18, 1867, Madame Arabella Goddard played at the Monday Popular Concert, for the first time in public, Book Eight of Mendelssohn's "Lieder ohne Worte," a few days before its publication by the firm.* This was one of a number of the Posthumous works of the composer, the remainder of which were issued in the early part of the

---

* The price paid for the English copyright of this was £200, a contrast to the fact that the first book was printed at the expense of the author.

following year; among these were "The Reformation Symphony," the "Cornelius March," the "Trumpet Overture," a Sextet for pianoforte and stringed instruments, a number of pianoforte pieces, including the two Sonatas, the "Ave Maria," and Vintage Song from "Loreley."

The further publications of the year 1868 include "The Psalter, pointed and adapted to the Ancient Ecclesiastical Chant," by W. T. Best; the continuation of Novello's Choir Book; Ouseley's Eight Anthems; the Anglican Hymn Book, edited by the Rev. Robert Corbet Singleton and Dr. E. G. Monk; besides a large number of Instrumental and Vocal Works, sacred and secular, by Henry Smart, W. J. Westbrook, J. B. Calkin, Henry Hiles, John Goss, A. R. Gaul, Chopin, and many others. Cheap editions of Dr. S. S. Wesley's compositions, of which Novello & Co. had acquired the copyright, were also issued.

The great Handel Festival was held again in 1868, at the Crystal Palace. Efforts were being made to induce the Government to provide some substantial support for the Royal Academy of Music, then the only musical training institution in London. The professors had given strong evidence of their interest in the school by the many personal sacrifices which they had made to help to keep it in a state of efficiency. Among the noteworthy events outside the operations of the firm, having a distinct congeniality of aim, may be named the series of Concerts of Modern Music given in 1870 by Willem Coenen at Hanover Square Rooms, at which new works by Brahms, Svendsen, Mackenzie, and others were heard for the first time.

Hymns and Carols.

Mention should be made of the publication, in July, 1869, of the first volume of Mr. J. Barnby's "Hymns with Tunes," a collection of his contributions to various Hymnals, with some new compositions, appearing in this volume for the first time. In these the composer's peculiar talent found fittest expression, and the encouragement received by him prompted him to compile a second volume of like character, which, however, did not appear until January, 1883, fourteen years after the first.

The first series of Stainer and Bramley's Christmas Carols appeared in November, 1867. The second in 1871. The year 1870 also saw the production of many original Organ Compositions by Barnby, Best, Calkin, Collin, Fieldwick, Gladstone, Hainworth, Hiles, Jekyll, Lemmens, Léfèbure - Wély, Liszt, Mendelssohn, Ouseley, Prichard, Sangster, Silas, Henry Smart, C. E. Stephens, Miss Stirling, Thorne, and Wesley ; Best's "Studies for the Pedals"; the first parts of Spark's "Organist's Quarterly Journal": the "Harmonium Treasury," arrangements by J. W. Elliott; pieces by Westbrook; vocal and instrumental works by Barnby, Garrett, Goss, Pinsuti, Rubinstein, Silas, &c.; a number of pianoforte classics in the popular octavo form; a uniform octavo edition of Mendelssohn's pianoforte works, and many of the vocal and instrumental compositions of Henry Hiles, including his "Fayre Pastorel." Barnby's sacred idyl "Rebekah" was also published this year. In *The Musical Times* Dr. W. Pole told the "Story of Mozart's Requiem," and other noteworthy articles kept the interest of the paper bright and vigorous.

114 CHEAP MUSIC. 1868-1877.

The first direct association of the name of Charles Gounod with the house took place in 1871, when the copyrights of several of his compositions, vocal and instrumental, such as the "Saltarello," written for the Philharmonic Society; "De Profundis," "Gallia,' "There is a green hill," and other works, were purchased and printed by the firm.

"The Hymnary, a Book of Church Song," was the earliest publication of 1872. This large and valuable collection of Ancient and Modern Hymn Tunes contained compositions by most of the foremost composers, both native and foreign, of the time. The music for the National Music Meetings, held at the Crystal Palace in June and July; the publication of Bach's "Passion according to St. John," and the performance of the work at Hanover Square Rooms; the music for the Thanksgiving Service at St. Paul's Cathedral for the recovery of the Prince of Wales; the Festival Te Deum Laudamus, and Domine salvam fac Reginam, by Sullivan; a collection of Opera Choruses in octavo size; and Christmas carols at a penny each, constituted a portion of the work of the firm, and the later additions to the catalogue. Mendelssohn's "St. Paul" was given this year on St. Paul's Day, in St. Paul's Cathedral, for the first time.

The Cathedral Psalter, pointed for chanting by the Rev. S. Flood Jones, the Rev. J. Troutbeck, Dr. Stainer, Messrs. J. Turle and J. Barnby, and the issue of a new edition of Monk and Ouseley's Psalter, already in extensive use, testified to the increase of choral services beyond the confines of the Cathedrals. The substitution of the "Benedicite" for the "Te Deum," at morning service during Advent and Lent was becoming general, and the institution of Choral Communion at St. Paul's Cathedral had been the means of awakening attention to the matter elsewhere, and so calling into existence a larger literature of music for the purpose than had heretofore been available.

One of the peculiar features of the music of the year was what might be called an epidemic of Marches. Nearly every publisher, yielding to the demand for this form of composition, issued pieces by various composers. A long list of Marches for the organ, supplemental to those for the pianoforte, was added to the publications of the month of December. The following year the mania took another form—the reproduction of tarantellas, minuets, gavottes, sarabandes, bourrées, &c.

The Musical Times, which at its beginning, in 1844, was a modest periodical of eight pages, had expanded its bulk so that at times it had been extended to twenty-four pages. In January, 1868, it was permanently enlarged to thirty-two pages, and the price was raised from three-halfpence to twopence. Reviews of new music, accounts of important musical events, and articles upon the art were made the subject of even more prominent consideration than before. The journal increased largely in circulation and influence. The space accorded to the records of choral performances throughout the United Kingdom and the Colonies, which had always characterised the journal as a "Singing Class Circular," was augmented, and its usefulness and value proportionately extended. The series of most valuable articles on "The music of the English Church," by G. A. Macfarren, was continued, and the names of writers in the paper bore testimony to the honest endeavour made to carry out every promise to show that the journal was "guided solely by the interest of the art in its most intellectual form." James William Davison, himself a tower of strength, contributed some valuable critical articles; the writings of Henry C. Lunn, whose keen-sightedness in matters of art, genial manner of writing, and excellent literary style always made his contributions attractive and distinguishable, whether they were signed or not; together with an excellent and readable course of articles on the Incidents in the life of Beethoven, by S. M. Hayley, form the chief literary articles of the paper during 1868. Meantime the house was also active, not only in the prosecution of such labours as legitimately belong to a publishing firm, but also in those matters which pertain to the advancement of art.

The Birmingham Festival of 1870 brought forward some important works, such as the oratorio "St. Peter," by Benedict; "Nala and Damayanti," by Hiller, &c. *The Musical Times* announces the first instalment of a fine edition of Handel's Coronation and Chandos Anthems, with additional accompaniments for a modern orchestra, by E. Silas; Best's arrangement of "The Messiah," including Mozart's additions, in octavo, price two shillings; the first of Novello's Octavo Editions of the Operas, Beethoven's "Fidelio";[*] the prospectus of "A New

---

[*] The prospectus of Novello's Edition of Operas was inserted in the August number of *The Musical Times*. It was the first announcement of a cheap edition of operas in octavo size.

Hymnal," and the announcement of J. W. Elliott's
"National Nursery Rhymes," with sixty-five illustrations by the Brothers Dalziel. The copyrights of
Costa's Serenata "The Dream"; of Goss's edition of
Haydn's Canzonets; of Spohr's Opera "Jessonda,"
English and German words; of Callcott's arrangements from Spohr's "Last Judgment," and glees for
three voices, with collections of part-songs, by
Goldschmidt, Hatton, Walter Macfarren, Reay, Henry
Smart; Church music, by Steggall, Smart, Chipp,
Hopkins, &c.; and "Cassell's Choral Music," edited
by Henry Leslie, became the property of Novello,
Ewer & Co. in January. The earliest appearance of
the name of Berthold Tours, associated with the house,
is indicated by the publication of six of his Songs in
1870. In December it was announced that *The
Musical Times*, unaided by any advertisement, "had
reached a circulation of 14,000." A supplement
issued with this number—the first of the kind—contained much interesting matter concerning musical
affairs. The publications of the firm included the
commencement of the series entitled "Novello's
Octavo Anthems," by the greatest modern composers, together with many by ancient writers, called
forth by the preference shown by the musical public
for the small scores over the separate vocal parts.
Many of the Anthems in the list could only be obtained before in the large and comparatively expensive folio size. There was also a complete uniform
edition of Mendelssohn's Songs, edited, and in part
translated, by Natalia Macfarren.

The Musical Times contained articles by the editor,
Henry C. Lunn; occasional contributions by Joseph

Bennett (this time being the earliest period of his association with the journal, to which, in later years, his writings added so much value), J. C. Lobe, Joseph Green, G. A. Macfarren, W. A. Barrett, John Stainer, and others. The circulation and the usefulness of the publication steadily increased. A new Music Store was opened in America, at No. 751, Broadway, New York, "the rapid growth of musical taste in America necessitating this step."

The first Bristol festival was held in October, 1873; orchestral concerts had been given at the Alexandra Palace, and the progress of music was in every way encouraging; John Hullah had been appointed Inspector of music in training colleges; the National Training School of Music was commenced; scholarships were added to those already existing at the Royal Academy; and attempts were made to improve the character of the music given at the Promenade Concerts, by the introduction of classical music and oratorios, of which Messrs. Riviere and Barnby were the conductors.

Miss Agnes Zimmermann's edition of Beethoven's sonatas; a "School for the Harmonium," by King Hall; "The Song of Destiny," by Brahms; a number of Masses adapted from the Latin to the words of the English ritual as Communion Services for use in the Anglican Church, by Gounod, Hummel, Farmer, and Schubert; with oratorios, cantatas, &c., by Bach, Gade, Handel, Macfarren, Schumann, Smart, and Sullivan; the "Selection" for the Handel Festival of 1874; some of the publications for the festivals at Liverpool and Leeds, with other compositions of minor import, were the work of the house for the year. The *Musical Times* contained, among other correspondence and interesting notices, a number of letters for and against the "Moveable Do," *àpropos* of John Hullah's report on music in the training colleges.

In 1875 the Hanover Square Rooms were closed as concert rooms, after an existence of over one hundred years. An admirable sketch of the history of the rooms from 1774, by Mr. Henry C. Lunn, appeared in *The Musical Times*. Elsewhere the reduction of the number of available concert rooms was lamented, because it was felt that a time would come when it would be advantageous to have a few smaller concert rooms for the performance of music on a lesser scale than it had then grown to be the fashion to give. For a time small concerts were neglected. Choral services were on the increase, and, following the example of one or two leaders of musical practice, certain additions to the Service of the Church were adopted in many instances. Introits — though no provision is made for their introduction by the rubric — and Offertory Sentences were sung without complete regard to the direction that the choir shall sing the sentences after the priest has said them. The "Agnus Dei" and "Benedictus qui venit in nomine Domini," following the direction of the unrepealed prayer-book of Edward the Sixth, also were interpolated in the new settings of the Communion Service.

During this year the "Sunlight of Song," a collection of sacred and moral poems, with original music by eminent English composers, profusely illustrated by the Brothers Dalziel, was called into existence by the demand for Sunday music, then on the increase. A number of settings of the Benedictus, by various writers, intended to be used with those services still retained in the Church, for which the original composer had only furnished a setting of the Jubilate; some additional chants for the Benedicite, used in place of the Te Deum; a new edition of Hawkins's "History of Music," and a large number of lesser pieces were issued from the press.

With the intention of producing work equal, if not superior, to that of foreign firms, who for some time past had taken the lead in the matter, the services of a number of expert German engravers from Leipzig were engaged. The beauty and finish of the work done by these artists, as shown in the edition of the full scores of modern oratorios, cantatas, symphonies, &c., was acknowledged on all sides, and the firm was enabled to establish, as it were, a school of art in this particular department, which has not been without important results outside the domain of the house.

In addition to the importation of foreign music, which formed part of the business, the house undertook the duty of making more extensively known to the British public the cheap editions published by the celebrated firm of Peters, of Leipzig, an edition which was confessedly based upon the inventions and suggestions made by the house of Novello.

The publication for the year 1876 of a "Dictionary of Musical Terms," edited by John Stainer, M.A., Mus. Doc., and W. A. Barrett, Mus. Bac.; some Sol-fa editions of Anthems by various composers, and some of Mendelssohn's works, translated by

Enlargement of "The Musical Times." 121

W. G. McNaught; Jackson's "Choral Songs for School and Home," "A Theoretical and Practical Treatise on the Organ," by F. Archer; the music to an English version of the tragedy of "Alcestis, by Henry Gadsby; Carl Engel's "Musical Myths and Facts," indicates the cosmopolitan character which the business had now assumed. The city office was removed in June from the Poultry to new premises, 80 and 81, Queen Street, Cheapside, and a further enlargement of the popular periodical *The Musical Times* was determined upon. This determination was carried out in January, 1877, when the paper was increased to 48 pages, and the price was raised to threepence. The value of the periodical as the record of passing events was largely increased, and its interesting character was proportionately enlarged. The change was duly appreciated, and once more the head of the house, in showing that he had moulded circumstances to his will, and had not been wholly moulded to circumstances, could say with Horace: "Et mihi res, non me rebus, submittere conor."

CHAPTER V.

1878—1887

"All the choicest music of the kingdom."
Henry VIII., Act iv., Sc. 1.

IT is scarcely necessary further to trace, step by step, the publications of the house in order to show either its influence or its tendency; it continued to hold the unique position it had gained in the trade, and was also duly recognised as a power in Art. During the long course of years in which the firm had existed and laboured, it had never sought to interfere with others. It had preferred to work harmoniously with those who were apparently moving on parallel lines. Its labours had been imitated by many. It was its business to originate. When success was won, and the new paths were opened, others were free to enter upon them if they chose to do so; but the musical world was not insensible to the fact that they who had found out the way were the best guides in that way. Therefore, trust and confidence were continued to those who were proved to be best worthy. One by one many who entered the field as antagonists were compelled to retire from want of support on the part of the public. The favour with which the initial attempts of the house had been received had developed into confidence in, if not of affection for, the later publications. Not only in Great Britain, but in the Colonies, in America, in every place on the habitable globe where English was spoken or music practised and cultivated, Novello's publications were always certain of a welcome, due not only to their cheapness, but to their accuracy, beauty, and superior quality of production. These qualities were attained through much care and forethought, and often by means of considerable outlay of capital in directions which were designed to augment the advantages offered to the consumer. At the beginning of the first decade of the Queen's reign, when Alfred Novello had succeeded in proving to the musical public his object in business, he was dependent on many outside trades—engravers, type-music compositors, printers, bookbinders, &c.—each with peculiarities which had to be considered. When the exorbitant dues demanded for all press-work, and the arbitrary rules of the printing trade forced him into a business of which he had only the customary outside knowledge, it was hoped by his opponents that his design of making music cheap for the public would come to nought, and his attempt to court the confidence of the lovers of music would be completely rejected. On the contrary, it served as the foundation of his fortune and as the medium through which he could more successfully carry out his cherished design. He was enabled, as has been already shown, to introduce new founts of type, and so to make the improvements which were so much wanted and which have since become a necessity to all lovers of music. When the business of publishing was removed to Berners Street, and the old premises in Dean Street were no longer required in that capacity, the room for the printing office was extended, the business was enlarged and became more general in character. Besides the considerable amount of work required for the production of their own special publications, the firm had made such arrangements that they could undertake the printing of books, magazines, newspapers, illustrated catalogues, circulars at the ordinary type presses and machines, as well as maps, plans, and all kinds of lithographic and colour printing.

The binding of their books, no inconsiderable trade item, was now under their own management, suitable premises for the purpose having been taken at Nos. 111 and 113, in Southwark Street, then a new way connecting by a direct line Blackfriars Road with the High Street, Borough, Southwark. A little later a third house, No. 115, was added to meet the necessities of the business, and now, with the exception of making the paper which is required, and of which large quantities are daily consumed, every branch of the business is under one control, so that the firm is enabled to secure a complete production of the works issued, and be themselves responsible for a uniform degree of excellence throughout.

More intimate relations with America were secured through the agency of Messrs. Ditson & Co., of Boston, New York, and Philadelphia; and, a little later (1884), by the establishment of a branch under the firm's own direction at 129, Fifth Avenue, New York. The American people, guided in their musical tastes by several admirable musicians, had cultivated the higher forms of musical expression such as are supplied in symphonies and other orchestral works, as well as in choral singing. The number of singing societies has gradually increased during the last ten years, innumerable institutions in various parts of the States, emulating the worthy example set by the Handel and Haydn Society of Boston, follow the footsteps of the leaders of the old country, under such earnest and enterprising chiefs as Theodore Thomas and his able lieutenant, W. L. Tomlins, of Chicago, Carl Zerrahn, and many others. Music has made great advances in America. Nearly every town has its own choir, by whose means music, both sacred and secular, is studied and advanced. There are many voices of exceptional beauty among the people, whose charms are acknowledged by the whole civilised world. Albani, Kellogg, Cary, Ella Russell, Osgood, Antoinette Sterling, Edward Scovel, W. J. Winch, Myron Whitney, and others, whose fame is European, are American by birth, but their talents belong as much to England as to their own country. Composers are not wanting in all departments, and the excellence displayed in the compositions of Dudley Buck and musicians of like *calibre* prove that their minds are moved by the highest aspirations. Therefore the interest in choral music is rapidly developing, and the characteristic qualities of enterprise and energy are being applied to all branches of musical art.

In England also new choral societies were established not only in the country, but in the suburbs of London. Many of them, directed by most competent and skilful musicians, succeeded in doing good work more or less missionary-like in character, inasmuch as they were showing to those unacquainted with them the master-works of ancient and modern composers, the copies of the compositions pouring from the press in vast quantities as required.

For educational purposes, in another direction, a valuable series of works, "Novello, Ewer & Co.'s Music Primers," containing practical treatises on various subjects, edited by Dr. Stainer, and contributed by Ernst Pauer, W. H. Cummings, Dr. Bridge, James Higgs, Rev. J. Troutbeck, Berthold Tours, King Hall, Alberto Randegger, E. Prout, John Curwen, the editor, and other eminent musicians, began to appear in 1877, and was being constantly added to.

In 1881 attention was first drawn in the pages of *The Musical Times* to the genius of Antonín Dvořák, a musician since become better known to Englishmen by means of his compositions, brought to a hearing through the medium of the firm and published by them a little later in time. The publication of an English edition of his masterly work, the setting of the words of the ancient hymn "Stabat Mater Dolorosa," placed the musical world face to face with a man of genius, who, but for the encouragement offered by the house, might have "wasted his sweetness on the desert air" of limited appreciation for a lengthened period. His original melodic powers, his bold and massive use of orchestral tone, place him high in the ranks of those who, by their use of developed means, represent the spirit of the age exemplified in music, and make their labours a pattern for example and imitation.

It was intended that the "Stabat Mater" should be included in the programme of the Birmingham Festival [1882], but the arrangements with the German publisher could not be concluded in time for this, and the house was consequently enabled to give the London Musical Society the opportunity of performing this great work for the first time in England.

Many notable changes were brought about by the aid of the firm, most of which were made at exactly the right time. Some may possibly have been in advance of the time. The introduction of men's voice services in St. Paul's Cathedral and Westminster Abbey does not appear to have been very extensively imitated throughout the country, though provision of compositions was made by many writers; but an edition of Christmas Carols for men's voices, published in December, was gladly welcomed. Music was now so largely cultivated that there was quite a run upon the Primer Series, and a new industry among musicians, that of teaching by correspondence, had apparently been productive of favourable results. In the December number of *The Musical Times*, besides the advertisements of the transactions of musical societies, associations, choral classes, of voices and organists wanting and wanted, and address cards of musicians, there is a list of many graduates in music, &c., who offer their help to teach candidates harmony, counterpoint, orchestration, &c., by post. There was quite a passion for examination, and most of the recognised musical institutions made arrangements for granting certificates of proficiency in singing and playing. In addition to the pianoforte, the violin was now more extensively studied than heretofore. The use of that instrument was not confined to the sterner sex, but ladies, discovering that the violin was neither ungraceful nor unbecoming, entered most ardently upon the study of an instrument which was picturesque enough to have justified painters in pourtraying its employment by St. Cecilia herself, the patron saint of the art.

The year 1882 saw many changes amongst the old established musical institutions. The Sacred Harmonic Society was dissolved after an existence of half-a-century, and its fine library sold to the Royal College of Music,* a new institution, the outcome of the efforts made to establish a National Training School for Music, which was being formed at this time, and which, thanks to the great energy and active interest taken in the cause of music by H.R.H. the Prince of Wales, was established in the year after. In 1882 the Duke of Edinburgh wrote to Sir George Grove, *àpropos* of the foundation of the Royal College of Music, a letter, a quotation from which, as a high testimony of the operations of the firm, will not be out of place in speaking of the occurrences of the year:—

" I shall be glad if you will see Mr. Littleton, the head of the firm of Novello & Co., and mention to him the Royal College of Music, the establishment of which the Prince of Wales and I have so much at heart. No house has done such service to music in England as that eminent firm has by their editions of Handel, and their numerous publications of new works by native composers."

* The portrait of Handel, by Denner, the fine portrait of Dr. Arne, by Zoffany, and the double portrait picture of Joah Bates and his wife (Sarah Harrop), by Coates, together with the Vauxhall statue of Handel, were purchased from the Society by Mr. Littleton. The statue of Handel was the first important work of Roubiliac, the monument to Handel in Westminster Abbey was his last.

Among other events of the year it may be well to mention that Wagner's last work, "Parsifal," had been performed at Bayreuth for the first time; and a kind of concert-recital of a large selection from the work was given at the Albert Hall in the following year. A series of representations of "Der Ring des Nibelungen," by Wagner, at Her Majesty's Theatre, by German artists, under the direction of Herr Angelo Neumann, had been artistically successful but financially unprofitable. A season of German Opera at Drury Lane also saw the production of other operas by Wagner.

The oratorio, or rather the sacred trilogy, "The Redemption," for which Messrs. Novello paid the composer the unprecedented sum of £4,000, was produced at the Birmingham Festival, and met with an extraordinary reception each time it was presented.* It formed the chief attraction at the festivals in some of the larger towns, and when it was performed for the first time in London, at the Royal Albert Hall, it was said that nearly twelve thousand persons were present. Gounod called it the "work of his life," and popular opinion confirmed his statement.

Besides the Festival at Birmingham, which was one of the most successful on record, having attracted as many as 18,507 persons, and produced no less a sum than £15,011 3s. 8d., the Hereford Festival was no less proportionately fortunate. A new cantata, "The Shunammite," by Dr. Garrett; Molique's "Abraham," and a new setting of Collins's "Ode to the Passions,"

---

* A very liberal proportion of this sum was paid by the Festival committee, in consideration of the right of the first performance of the work.

"The Redemption."

by Alice Mary Smith (Mrs. F. Meadows White), besides the perennial Oratorios "Elijah" and "The Messiah," all testified to the spirit of musical enterprise in the committee of the festival in "the little city on the Wye." The cantata by Alice Mary Smith was the first work written by a lady which had been produced on so important an occasion. Copies of these compositions were prepared at Novello's press, and distributed throughout the land, from "Maidenkirk to John o' Groats," and from "Berwick-on-Tweed to Penzance."

Gounod's "Redemption" was performed at Westminster Abbey in March, 1883, and has been given in many of the most important provincial towns, as well as in Brussels, Paris, Vienna, Berlin, Rotterdam, Melbourne, and many towns in America. In the last-named country it had been ruled that it could not be performed with orchestration arranged from the pianoforte score, according to a common, but not over honest practice with popular works. This ruling called the attention of the American people once more to the weakness of the law as affecting international copyright. Many difficulties exist which have yet to be smoothed over, and it is hoped that the day is not far distant when it will be deemed reasonable, on the part of people of all countries, to be asked to contribute something towards the rewards given to brain workers, whose efforts are a source of profit to them. It is not considered unfair to expect payment for works of the hand or the produce of the farm—international treaties take care of such matters. A new Alfred Novello is wanted to agitate for the adjustment of these taxes upon knowledge producers.

At Worcester, in 1881, a new cantata, "The Bride," by Alexander Campbell Mackenzie, was produced, and awakened the keenest interest on behalf of the composer. In the following year he produced "Jason" for Bristol; and in 1883 his fine opera "Colomba" was performed at Drury Lane Theatre by the Carl Rosa Opera Company. This was felt to be the work of one of whose labours the highest expectations might be formed, and when, in 1884, the "Rose of Sharon" was produced at Norwich, it was accepted as a realisation of the hopes entertained of his genius. The grand duet from the fourth act of "Colomba" was selected for performance at a State concert on the 27th June, 1883, the first time for many years that the work of a native musician had been so honoured. It would seem as if the golden age of the great Queen Elizabeth was reviving in favour of musicians in the days of the greater Queen Victoria. Changes of great importance were taking place rapidly, not only in the feeling as regards home-grown art, but also in the treatment of artists. English composers were taking high rank in the estimation of their own countrymen, and were honoured by the performance of their works abroad. The names of Stanford, Sullivan, Goring Thomas, Cowen, Hubert Parry, Prout, and others were being made as familiar on the Continent as at home. English singers were engaged for performances in foreign cities. As English publishers, Novello, Ewer & Co. thought it a duty not only to encourage rising merit, but also to reproduce works which might bear witness of their desire to make known some of the monuments of foreign research.

Literary Publications.

With this view Otto Jahn's "Life of Mozart" and Philipp Spitta's "Life of Bach" were produced in an English dress. The first was translated by Pauline D. Townshend, the second by Clara Bell and J. A. Fuller Maitland. The care and attention paid to the production of these works as specimens of printing, independent of other qualities, could scarcely be recuperated by the sale. It is, therefore, reasonable to assume that the house was moved in the matter by considerations of art rather than by any hope of profit. Equally excellent as examples of typography, and no less valuable in degree as a contribution to musical literature, was Carl Engel's "Researches into the Early History of the Violin-Family," which is included in the publications of the year. The catalogues of the house assumed important proportions in every department. The new works written for, or brought out at the festivals at Gloucester and Leeds, with the selection for the Handel Festival of 1883, conducted by Mr. Manns for the first time, were also printed and published. Sir Michael Costa, who had directed the triennial performances since their institution in 1857, was stricken with illness, from which he never recovered.

This year a further attempt was made to establish a National Opera, and a sketch of the objects proposed to be effected was commented upon in the *Times* newspaper. The building on the Thames Embankment, the foundation stone of which was laid by the Duke of Edinburgh in 1875, had remained unfinished and deserted for a long time. It was now intended to complete it, and open it for the purpose for which it was constructed. The capital, £70,000, was stated to have been furnished, and it was expected to be opened for the season of 1884. This scheme was, however, never carried out, and shortly afterwards the structure was swept away and a new street formed on the site.

Fifty years or so before, John Braham lost a fortune in building St. James's Theatre for operatic purposes. Balfe made an attempt in 1841 to establish a National Opera at the Lyceum Theatre, and nearly twenty years later an English Opera Company at Covent Garden Theatre enjoyed a short run of success. The project seems to have had a periodical fascination over speculative minds, which may continue to arise until the thing is actually a *fait accompli*.

The steady progress of business, guided by well-judged ventures, was productive of more substantial results. At the beginning of 1884 the firm of Novello acquired the copyright of the additional accompaniments written at various times by Sir Michael Costa, for use in the performance of many works by Handel, either for the Sacred Harmonic Society or the Handel Festival. Antonín Dvořák was invited to England by the firm, in conjunction with the Philharmonic Society, and conducted his own setting of the "Stabat Mater," and other works.

The Sacred Harmonic Society in its reconstructed state, with W. H. Cummings as the successor of Charles Hallé as conductor, was doing good work; and the suburban choral societies were modestly labouring to extend a knowledge of the best works among their subscribers and patrons, which had not been previously generally available. In the Provinces, in the Colonies, and even in certain Continental towns, English music was heard and English artists welcomed. Novello's editions were known all over the world.

The recurrence of the Birmingham Festival in 1885 brought forth M. Gounod's second Sacred Trilogy, "Mors et Vita," Dvořák's "Spectre's Bride," Cowen's "Sleeping Beauty," and Mackenzie's Violin Concerto, all published by Novello, Ewer & Co.

It is only necessary to mention, as belonging to this year, the change in the course of the Handel Festival in order to make it coincident with the date of the year of the bi-centenary of the composer's birth at Halle in 1685. The Exhibition of Inventions and Music at South Kensington added not a little to the knowledge of ancient and modern music, European and Asiatic, to that which was already possessed by students. A certain degree of impetus was given to the study of choral singing by the prizes offered by the committee in connection with the Exhibition. Societies from Dover, Birmingham, Leicester, Nottingham, Rhondda, Preston, Burslem, Hanley, Vale of Clwyd, Sheffield, Liverpool, Manchester, Chesterfield, Portsmouth, Redhill, and certain of the suburbs of London competed, and it was hoped that the like competitions would be made of annual occurrence. The encouragements thus offered would doubtless tend to the improvement of choral singing all over the country. At all events, it would show the extent to which the practice of united singing had spread, and the advantage to art would be considerable.

England was certainly taking a foremost place in directing certain phases of musical opinion, and other nations were following where she led.

The first performance of Gounod's "Mors et Vita" in Paris did not take place until May 22, 1886. The composer conducted, and the soloists were Madame Kraus, Madame Conneau (who sang at the Royal Albert Hall when she was in London in 1870), M. Faure, and Mr. Edward Lloyd, who went to France expressly to sing the tenor music.

At the Antwerp Exhibition, English musicians and *litterateurs* were invited to express their views upon the subject of educational matters in music, in order that a better understanding of the general principles which guided all right-minded men might be established by the interchange of opinions upon matters of common employment. So the year 1886 was reached.

The list of events in the last completed year of the record now before the reader need not be dwelt upon, beyond recording the fact that all the important new works produced at the highly successful Leeds Festival were published by the firm. These included Dvořák's "St. Ludmila," Mackenzie's "Story of Sayid," Stanford's "Revenge," and Sullivan's "Golden Legend."

The establishment of the new series of concerts, entitled Novello's Oratorio Concerts, begun in the autumn of 1885, under the auspices of the firm, for the purpose of performing new or little known works, brought forward Dr. A. C. Mackenzie in a manner which testified to his ability as a conscientious interpreter of music of an exalted character, and served emphatically to show that he could take as high a position as a conductor of choral and orchestral music as he had already done as a composer. Many new works, which might not otherwise have been brought to a hearing so soon, were presented to a London audience for the first time in admirable style; and notwithstanding the enormous amount of work achieved within a very short time, the performances were excellent and elicited the highest praise. The result was due to the energy of the conductor, and the loyal enthusiasm and indefatigable efforts of the choir. With the exception of "Mors et Vita," no work was twice given in the two seasons of six concerts each. Among many notable performances, especial mention may be made of the "Rose of Sharon," "St. Elizabeth," "St. Ludmila," "Golden Legend," Spohr's "Calvary," and the Choral Symphony; a finer rendering than that of the last work can hardly be imagined.

The special performance of "Mors et Vita" in the Royal Albert Hall, by the command, and in the presence of the Queen, warmed the loyalty and raised the hearts of those who remembered how constant a supporter of music and of worthy musicians Her Majesty had been. The highest hopes were entertained for the future of music, and as in the course of the year following (1887) the Queen would have completed the fiftieth year of her reign, it was the wish of all who loved the art that it might once more enjoy the sunshine of her personal patronage and favour.

The visit of Franz Liszt to England, at the invitation of the head of the firm, was one of the many notable events associated with the history of the house. He had, over and over again, refused the offer of large sums of money for an artistic engagement in London, but he readily accepted the invitation of Mr. Henry Littleton—supported, as it was, by his friend and pupil Walter Bache and others—to be present at the performance of his Oratorio "St. Elizabeth."

Musicians and amateurs were alike gratified by the opportunity of seeing, and in a few instances of hearing, the great Master, whose influence in the world of art was so powerful and extensive.

His short sojourn in London, one of the last acts of a busy and eventful life, was remembered and referred to by him as full of pleasant memories. He expressed his intention, should his life be spared, of renewing in the following year a visit which had afforded so much that was agreeable to him. This intention was also not to be carried out. His death created a regret as sincere as the welcome accorded to him during his stay in England.

Time and space do not permit of much more reference to the events of the year. All that now is wanting to complete the record of the history of the five decades which have passed since our Queen became supreme ruler in the land may be told in "free speech and fearless," showing that "truth hath better deeds than words," even though those words relate chiefly to the progress of a house of business.

When Alfred Novello commenced his operations, having "a couple of parlour windows and a glass door, with a few title-pages bearing composers' names of sterling merit, and Vincent Novello as editor,"

The Labours of the House. 141

he little dreamed of the extent to which his enterprise would reach. That "simple parlour shop" became "the germ of the mart for supplying England—nay, the world—with highest class music."

The few engraved plates, paid for out of hard earnings and careful savings by Vincent Novello, became the nucleus of an enormous property, the details of which are no less astonishing than interesting. From the small beginning in 1811, when Vincent Novello, supported by his own energy, and encouraged only by his own family, issued his first publication, the business has expanded into what is probably the largest of its kind in the world, and gives employment to a staff of upwards of 450 persons.

Some idea of the extent of the present catalogue may be gathered from the fact that it includes no less than 10,550 separate works in octavo size alone, ranging in price from one penny to four shillings. There are also 10,236 pub ications in folio, or ordinary music size. To this list may be added a very large number of works—nearly fifty—in full score, a list unprecedented in the annals of publishing in England.

The retirement of Mr. Henry Littleton from the active direction of the firm at the beginning of 1887 introduced a fourth generation to the charge and conduct of the business. In the full possession of manly power and mental vigour, he can enjoy the ease he has earned by a long course of industrious labour; and if ever just cause of pride existed, it accompanies him in his retirement. He this year completes half-a-century of association with the music-trade, exactly concurrent with the years of the Queen's reign, during forty-six years of which he has been associated with the house of Novello. He attained his position as head of the firm by his honesty of purpose, shrewdness, foresight, and sound commercial judgment, and has helped to build a business which is without an equal. His singleness of purpose and integrity of action not only have had considerable influence in his own days, but may stand as a model for all time.

Nearly every one of our young British composers has received sympathy and encouragement from the firm; and in most instances their first compositions have been made known to the world through the house. English music itself owes a debt of gratitude to the house of Novello, as the position it has now gained would certainly have been retarded many years had it not been for the efforts of those who have directed the operations of the firm. Church music has been led to great improvements, choral societies have been established and nourished, popular taste in music has been guided and directed, and it is therefore with a special amount of gratification that those who believe in a great future for music will heartily wish God speed to the present representatives of the firm of Novello, Ewer & Co., as having accomplished great work in the past, as doing good in the present, and as having the desire and the will to maintain the best traditions of the house in the future.

INDEX.

"An index to the story we late talked of."
Richard III., Act ii., Sc. 2.

"Acis and Galatea" . . 62	Arnold, Dr., of Winchester 95
Additional accompaniments 105, 116	,, Dr. S. (note) . . 56
Adeste Fideles 4	Arnold's Cathedral Music. 5, 7
Advance of Sacred Music . 89	"Athalie," Mendelssohn 97, 104
Advertisement duty removed 31, 59	"Ave Maria," ,, . 112
Albani, Madame 128	*Athenæum* Newspaper . 82
Albertazzi, Madame . . 21	*Atlas* ,, . 21
Albion Hall. 7	Attwood, Thomas . . 23, 81
"All among the Barley" . 59	,, Cathedral Music 81
Allcock, Dr. (note) . . . 56	Ayrton, Dr. 23
Allen, G. B. 95	
Allgemeine Musiklehre . 64	Bach, Spitta's life of . . 135
Amateur performances . 18	Bach's Christmas Oratorio 109
America 41, 63	,, "Passion" Music 104, 107, 108, 109, 110
,, Advance of Music in 125	,, "Passion" in St. Paul's 109
,, and England . . 125	,, "Passion" in Westminster Abbey . 107, 109
,, Intimate relations with 125	Bad taste in music . . . 27
,, "Redemption" in . 133	Baker, The Rev. Sir H. . 77
American branch. . . . 63	Balfe, M. W. 25, 136
Analytical programmes . 80	,, Moore's Irish Melodies 76
Ancient Ecclesiastic Chant, W. T. Best 112	Barnard's Select Church Music 6
Anglican Church . . . 5, 29	Barnby, J. . 86, 89, 95, 104, 107 108, 110, 111
,, Hymn Book . . 112	
Anthems and Part-songs . 85	,, Choir. . . . 96, 102
,, by S. Webbe . . 62	,, Hymns with tunes 113
,, for Parish Choirs 85	Barnett, John 25
,, by living composers 76	,, J. F. 110
Antient Concerts . . . 23, 25	Barrett, W. A. . . . 118, 120
Antwerp Exhibition . . 138	Bartholomew, Mrs. . . . 97
Archer, F., Treatise on the Organ 121	Bates, Joah, and his wife (note) 131
Argyll Rooms 25	"Battle of Prague" . . . 19
Armes, Dr. 95	Beethoven . 12, 40 93, 116

L

Index.

Beethoven, Choral Fantasia 106
,, ,, Symphony 106
,, Mass in C 12
,, Mass in D . . 35, 106
"Belshazzar," Handel . . 108
Benedicite Chants 85, 95, 120
Benedict, Jules . . 59, 79, 86
,, "St. Peter" 106
Benedictus 119
Bennett, Joseph . . 108, 118
,, W. Sterndale 20, 28, 86
Berlin Choir 62
Berlioz, Hector, on Instrumental conducting . 64
Berners Street 11
,, ,, Removed to 97
Best, W. T. 62, 81, 85, 86, 89, 95, 112, 113
,, Organ Works . 85
Bibles stereotyped . . . 10
Bi-centenary Festival of Handel's birth . . . 137
Birmingham Festival, 1870 116
,, ,, 1882 129
,, Town Hall Organ 12
Bishop, H. R. . . . 10, 23, 25
,, Glees . . . 85
,, "Seventh day" 13
Bookbinding 126
Boston Handel and Haydn Society 128
Bowley, R. K. 71
Boyce, Dr. W. . . 5, 7, 29
,, Cathedral Music 5, 55
Boyce, Dr. W. Own Services and Anthems . 34
Braham, John 136
Brahms, J. 112, 118
Bramley and Stainer's Carols 113
Bridge, J. F. 129
Bristol Tune Book . . 85, 87
Buck, Dudley 128
Button and Whitaker . . 8
Byron, Lord 20

Calkin, J. B. . . 95, 112, 113
"Calvary," Spohr . . . 139
Cary, A. L. 128

Cassell's Choral Music . . 117
Catalogues of Music . . . 41
Catel's Harmony 64
Cathedral Choir Book . . 48
,, Music, Boyce . 5
,, ,, Arnold . 5
,, Psalter . . . 114
,, Service, State of 8, 9
Causes of Prosperity . . . 126
Cecilian Society 7
Centenary editions of Handel's works 70
Chappell, S. Arthur . . 79
,, William, Popular Music 70
Charity Children 8
Cheap Classics 28
,, Concerts . . . 22, 103
,, Monday Evening Concerts 68
,, Music 43, 52, 53, 54, 55, 98
,, Publications . . . 22
Cherubini's Counterpoint . 64
Childe, Dr. 64
Choir and Chorus singing, by Fétis 64
Choir Benevolent Fund (note) 84
Choirs of all denominations 29
Chopin 112
Choral Classes 51
,, ,, increased 65, 69
Choral Communion at St. Paul's 115
,, Competitions . 137
,, Hand Book . . . 29
,, Missionary Character of 128
,, Music 117
,, Music Society, Ely Diocesan 94
,, Societies . . 29, 30
,, ,, ... 68, 69
,, ,, ... 128
,, Songs by Pearsall . 85
Chorus parts 81
,, singers, Scarcity of, in 1837 90
Christmas Carols . 76, 113, 130
Church, John 64

Index. 147

Church composition, Improvement of . . . 10
Church Services, octavo edition 83
City Office 69
Clarke, Dr. John, arrangements, Handel . . . 117
Clarke, Dr. John, of Cambridge 7
Clarke, J. Hamilton . 88, 95
,, Mary Cowden 62, 64, 86
Clarke-Whitfeld 7
Classes, Singing . . 8, 33, 40
Clementi 23
Clowes, Messrs. . . 10, 32, 33
Coenen, Willem 112
Colborne, Langdon . . . 86
Collection of Chants . . . 36
,, Motetts . . 4
,, Sacred Music 3
Collet, C. D. 84
Collin 113
"Colomba" 134
Commemoration of Purcell 9
Communion Services adapted 119
Compulsory Stamp . . 67, 92
Concerts of Modern Music 112
Controversy on Pitch . . 105
Cooper, George 89
,, ,, Manual . 91
,, ,, Organist's Assistant 91
Capes, J. M. 91
Copyright, International . 133
Cornelius March 112
Cornet-à-pistons . . . 42
Correspondence, Teaching by 130
Corri 21
Costa, Sir M. . . . 135, 136
Covent Garden Theatre . 25
Coventry and Hollier 11, 51, 98
Cowen, F. H. 134
Cramer 23
"Creation," Haydn . . 36, 66
,, Pocket edition 84
Creyghton 64
Croft, Dr. W., Anthems 5, 36
Crosby Hall 10, 97

Crotch's Elements . . . 64
Crotchet, The Golden . . 34
Cummings, W. H. . 129, 136
Curwen, J. 129
Crystal Palace, Sydenham 68
,, ,, Saturday Concerts 79

Dalziel Brothers . . 117, 119
Danby, John 4
Daunreuther, E. 110
Davison, F. 11
,, J. W. 11, 20, 77, 80, 116
Dean Street, Soho, No. 69 34
Death of Vincent Novello . 82
Deichmann, Carl 108
Dictionary of Musical Terms 120
Directorium Chori Anglicanum 58
Ditson & Co. 127
Divine Harmony, Weldon's 6
Domestic Music . . . 81, 90
Drury Lane 25
Duets 42
Duke of Edinburgh . 131, 135
,, Wellington . . . 24
Dvořák, Antonín . . . 129
Dvořák's Stabat Mater 129, 136
,, "St. Ludmila" . 138
,, "Spectre's Bride" 137

Earl of Wilton 107
Earliest Publications . . 4
Early Operations 11
Economics of Musick Printing 38
Edward the Sixth 119
Elevation of Taste . . . 28
"Elijah" . . . 51, 97, 107, 133
"Elizabeth, St.," Liszt 139, 140
Ella, John 80
Elliott, J. W. 113
,, Harmonium Treasury 113
Elliott, J. W., National Nursery Rhymes . . 117
Ellis, A. J. 129
Elvey, Dr. S. 86

L 2

Index.

	PAGE
Elvey, Sir G. J.	76
Ely Diocesan Church Music Society	94
Engel, C., Musical Myths.	121
,, Researches into the History of the Violin Family	135
English Composers	76 (note), 109, 119
,, Music	42
Engraved Plates	32
Enlargement of *The Musical Times*	121
Excise Duty on Paper	31, 60, 67, 92
Exeter Hall	42, 107
Exhibition of 1851	62, 68
,, Inventions and Music	137
Every-day Concerts	108
Every-night ,,	109
Ewer & Co.	97
Extension of the Business	127
Father Matthew	48
"Fayre Pastorel," Hiles	113
Festa, C.	40
Festival, Bristol, 1873	118
Fieldwick	113
Figured Bass	4
Fitzwilliam Music	4
Flood-Jones, the Rev.	114
Flute Music	17
Free and Easy Concerts	26
French Music	43
,, Pitch	105, 106
Fryer, Rev. Victor	3
Fuller-Maitland, J. A.	135
Gadsby, H., "Alcestis"	121
Gardiner, W., "Judah," an Oratorio	12
Garrett, G. M.	89, 95
Gaul, A. R.	112
Gauntlett, Dr.	86
Ged, W., and Stereotyping	10
Gem Fount	38
German Engravers	120
,, Opera at Drury Lane	132

	PAGE
Gibbons, O. (note)	6
Gibson, Milner	59
Gladstone, Dr.	113
Glee Hive	61, 85
,, Singing	20
Glees, Halfpenny	89
,, and Part-Songs	117
,, ,, Madrigals	104
Glover, Miss, Tetrachordal System	50
"God Save the King"	21
Goddard, Arabella	111
Golden Crotchet, The	34
Goldschmidt, O.	117
Goodban	42
Goring-Thomas	134
Goss, Sir John	10, 75, 86, 89, 112, 117
Gounod, Ch.	95, 104, 114
,, De Profundis	114
,, "Gallia"	114
,, "Mors et Vita"	138, 139
,, "Redemption"	132, 133
,, "Saltarello"	114
,, Seven Words	95
,, St. Cecilia Mass	95
,, "There is a Green Hill"	114
Government Prosecution Threatened	66
Great Britain and America	125
,, ,, the Colonies	41
Green, Joseph	118
Greene, Dr. M., Forty Select Anthems	5
Gregorian Music	50
Gresham Prize Anthems	10
Grisi, Madame	21
Grove, Sir George	79, 80, 131
Guildhall School of Music (note)	79
Guitar	20
Hackett, Miss	10
Hainworth	117
Hall, King	131
Hallé, Charles	136

Index.   149

	PAGE
Handel	23
,, College	79
,, Festival Contingent	90
,, "Jephtha" 36, 50, 104, 107	
,, "Judas Maccabæus" 36, 48, 62, 66	
,, "Messiah," 50, 57, 62, 66	
,, Pocket Edition of "The Messiah"	78
,, Works	23
,, Festival, 1857	71
,, ,, 1859	78
,, ,, 1862	86
,, ,, 1865	89
,, ,, 1868	112
,, ,, 1874	118
,, ,, 1884	136
,, Portrait and Statue (note)	135
Handel's "Acis and Galatea"	62
,, "Belshazzar"	108
,, Dettingen Te Deum	62
,, Full Scores	61, 80
,, "Israel in Egypt" 57, 78, 84, 108	
,, "Theodora"	109
,, Walsh's Plates	62
,, "Zadok the Priest"	62
Hanover Square Rooms 24, 25, 93, 112, 119	
Harmonium Treasury	117
Harmony, Catel on	64
Harp	20, 42
Harrison, Scores	7
Hatton, J. L., Part-Songs	117
Hauk, Minnie	105
Hawkins, Sir J.	63
,, History of Music	63, 120
Haydn	47
,, Canzonets	116
,, Masses	29
,, Seasons	106
Hayley, S. M.	120
Hayes, Philip	34
Hear my Prayer, Mendelssohn	97
Helmore, the Rev. T.	58, 64
Heming, Joseph	87

	PAGE
Hereford Festival	132
Her Majesty's Theatre	62, 88
Hesse, Adolph	95
Hickson, W. E.	8, 47
Higgs, James	129
Hiles, Henry	112, 113
Hiller, F., "Nala and Damayanti"	106
Hindrances to Progress	22
Holmes, Edward	35
Hood, Thomas	30
Hopkins, E. J.	76, 86
,, J. L.	86, 95
Horetzky	42
Horsley, W.	23
House of Commons	59
Hullah, John	9, 28, 106, 119
,, Classes	28
,, Part Music	9
Hymnary, The	114
Hymns	42
,, Ancient and Modern	77, 85, 87
Illustrated London News (note)	36
Imitations of Novello's editions	66
Improvements in Type music	32
Impulse in Singing	21
Increase of circulation of The Musical Times	78
Increase of interest in music	68
Infant's Prayer	58
Instrumental music	42
International Exhibition	84, 108
Introits or short Anthems	95, 119
Ions, Dr.	76
Irish Melodies, Moore's	76
"Israel in Egypt"	57, 78, 84, 108
Italian Music	43
,, Opera	24
Jacob's National Psalmody	12
Jackson, Dr., Bishop of London	75

Index.

Jackson of Masham	66
Jackson's Choral Songs	121
Jahn, Otto, Life of Mozart	135
Jekyll, C. S.	113
"Jephtha"	104, 107
"Jerusalem," Pierson	66
"Jessonda," Spohr	117
"John, Passion of," Bach.	114
Jones, Horace	79
Joule, Mr.	58
"Judah," an Oratorio	12
"Judas Maccabæus"	36, 48, 62, 66
Jullien and his band	68
Kellogg	128
Kelway	64
Kempton	64
King William the Fourth	9
Kirkmann	42
Knighthood for Alfred Novello	92
Lablache	27
Labours of the House	142
Lancashire Choral Societies	30
Le diapason normal	105
Léfebure-Wély	95
Lemmens, J.	95
Leslie's Choir	87
Leslie, Henry	103, 117
Licensing system	93
"Light of the World"	109
Linnet Waltz	19
Liszt, F.	20, 113, 139
,, "St. Elizabeth"	139
,, visit to England	139
Literary publications by the firm	135
Lithography	32
Littleton, Henry	30, 51, 69, 83, 92, 131
,, retirement	141
,, sole proprietor	92
Liverpool Festival, 1836	13
,, Philharmonic	59
London Concert Rooms	25
,, Musical Society, The	130
Lunn, Henry C.	87, 119
"Macbeth" Music	84
Macfarren, G. A.	28, 59, 86
,, W. C.	59
Macirone, George	64
Mackenzie, A. C.	134, 138
Mainzer's Compositions	30, 47
Mann, R.	86
Manns, August	79
Marches	115
Marston, Henry	104
Mayne, Sir R.	48
McNaught, W. G.	87, 121
Mendelssohn	13
,, "Athalie"	97, 104
,, Lieder	14
,, Lobgesang	29
,, Psalms	29
,, Songs	117
,, "St. Paul"	13, 36, 48, 57
"Messiah" published in numbers	35
Missionary character of Choral Societies	128
Monday Popular Concerts	79
Monk, E. G.	58, 76, 86, 112
,, W. H.	76, 86
,, and Ouseley's Psalter	86
Morley Thomas (note)	6
Motetts	6
Moveable Do	119
Mozart	24
,, additions to "Messiah"	116
,, and Haydn's Masses	29
Music for Men's voices	130
,, in National Schools	8
,, in the Theatres	25
,, playing cards	42
,, Primers	129
,, types	37, 38, 39
Musical Antiquarian Society	5, 9
,, Library	10
,, literary works	41
,, progress	23
,, Union	60
Musical Times.	33, 35, 39, 40, 48, 49, 50, 51, 56, 60, 75, &c.
Musical World	11, 40

Index. 151

"Nala and Damayanti" 106, 116
National Concerts . . . 62
,, Music Meetings . 114
,, Nursery Rhymes 117
,, Opera 135
,, Training School . 118
,, Training School for Music 131
Neglect of Music 19
Neukomm's Organ Book . 91
New Choral Societies . . 128
,, Music Store in America 118
Newspaper Stamp . . 31, 60
Nilsson, Christine . . . 106
Normal le diapason . . . 106
Norwich Sol-fa Ladder . . 50
Novello, Alfred 5, 6, 8, 10, 11, 22, 28, 29, 30, 31, 33, 37, 42, 49, 61, 65, 69, 71, 83, 92
Novello, Alfred, Circular for 1853 65
Novello, Alfred, relaxes business 69
Novello & Co. 83
,, Ewer & Co. . . . 98
,, Oratorio Concerts, new series . . . 108, 138
Novello, Cecilia 31
,, Clara . . . 31, 58
,, Sabilla . . 31, 64, 85
,, Vincent . 3, 9, 11, 23, 34, 39, 47, 58, 141
,, ,, Death of 82
,, ,, Memorial Window 86
,, v. Sudlow . . . 59
Novello's Cathedral Choir Book 58, 60
Novello's Cheap Oratorios . 57
,, ,, publications 29
,, Choir Book . . 112
,, Choral Hand Book 29
,, ,, Anthems 117
,, Octavo Choruses 65
,, ,, Hand Books 78
,, ,, Operas . 116
,, ,, Edition of Church Services . . . 83
,, Part-song Book . 58

Novello's Parish Choir Book 94
,, School Round Book 85
,, Standard Glee Book 88

Octavo Editions . . 33, &c.
Offertory Sentences . . . 119
Opera, Estimation of . . 25
,, Italian 24
,, Octavo Editions . 114
Oratorio Concerts 104, 107, 111
Oratorios and Church Music 53
Oratorios, Cheap . . . 66
,, Handel's . . 35
,, in Lent 25
,, Popular . . . 28
,, Full Scores . . 120
Organ Music 41, 81
,, Recitals at Liverpool 68
,, Sonatas, Mendelssohn 85
Organised Claque 27
Organist's Quarterly Journal 113
Original Compositions for the Organ 95
Osgood, Mrs. 128
Ouseley, Sir F. 65, 92
,, Eight Anthems 115

Page's Harmonia Sacra . . 5
Palestrina 91
Parado 42
Parry, C. H. Hubert . . . 134
"Parthenia" (note) . . . 6
"Passion St. John" . . . 114
,, St. Matthew" . 114
Pauer, E. 129
Pearl-Nonpareil Type . . 51
Penny Song Books . . . 26
Peters of Leipzig 120
Philanthropists and Singing 48
Philharmonic Concerts . . 21
,, Society 23, 25, 35, 82
Pianoforte Playing . . . 20
,, Thalberg . 21

Index.

Pocket Edition of "Creation" 84
Pocket Edition of "Israel" 84
Pole, Dr. W. 113
,, Mozart's Requiem 113
Popular Education . . . 22
,, Love for Music . 27
,, Music. 25
,, Musical Taste. . 21
,, Oratorios . . 28, 29
Portuguese Embassy . . 3
,, Hymn . . . 4
Posthumous Works, Mendelssohn 111
Poultry, No. 24 . . . 34, 37
Pratt's Collections . . . 91
Pre-Raphaelites 37
Preston, Publisher . . . 11
Prices paid for Mendelssohn's Book Eight of the Lieder. 111
Prices of Music 14
Prince of Wales 127
Printing Office in Dean Street 98
Prizes for Part-Songs . . 56
Provincial Festivals . . 28, 78
Prout, Ebenezer . . 129, 134
Psalmody Books 36
Psalter Noted 58
Publication of "St. Paul". 13
Publications of the year 1868 112
Purcell's Sacred Music 7, 29, 40
,, Commemoration. 11

Queen Adelaide 12
,, Anne. 31
,, Elizabeth . . . 134
,, Victoria 19, 56, 134, 139
Queen's, or West London Theatre. 24

Randall's Editions . . . 7
Randegger 110
"Redemption" Abroad . 133
,, in America . 133
,, in the Colonies 133

"Redemption" at Westminster Abbey . . . 133
Reduction of Prices . 52, &c.
,, ,, Public Press on 56
Reeves, Mr. Sims. . 105, 106
Reform 22
"Reformation" Symphony 104
Reinagle 42
Removal of City Office 69, 121
Revival of Church Feeling 30
Ribas 42
Rifle Volunteer Movement 81
Rimbault. 59
Roman Catholic Church . 29
"Rose of Sharon" . 134, 139
Rossini's "Stabat Mater" 29
,, First Performance 29
Royal Albert Hall 109, 111, 139
,, ,, Everyday Concerts. . . . 109
Royal Albert Hall, Everynight Concerts . . . 109
Royal Albert Hall, or Oratorio Concerts . . 109
Royal College of Music . 131
,, English Opera . . 88
"Rübezahl" 32
"Rule, Britannia" . . . 21
Rules of the Printing Trade 32
Russell, Ella 128

Sacred Harmonic Society 23, 28, 49, 71, 78, 104, 105, 131, 136
Sacred Music with English words 41
Sacred Music with Latin words 43
Sacred Music Warehouse . 34
Salomon 23
Scarcity of Chorus singers in 1837 90
School of Engraving . . 120
,, for the Harmonium 118
Scores, Oratorio full . . 120
Scovel, Edward 128
Senefelder, Aloys. . . . 32
Seymour Egerton, the Hon. 107

Index. 153

	PAGE
Sheet Music	32
Silas, E.	113, 116
Singing among the Workmen of Paris	47
,, by ear	26
,, Classes	8, 33
,, for the Million	30
,, Societies in the Country	137
Singleton, Rev. Corbet	112
"Slap-bang"	93
Smart, Henry	112, 113
,, Sir George	23
Smith, Alice Mary (Meadows White)	133
Soho, a Musical centre	13
,, Type Foundry	39
"Song of Destiny"	118
Spark, W.	113
Special Anthems for certain seasons	95
Spofforth, R.	40
Spohr's "Calvary"	139
,, "Jessonda"	117
,, "Last Judgment"	117
St. George's Hall	68
St. James's Hall	68
St. Martin's Hall	68
"St. Paul," Mendelssohn	29
St. Paul's, London	9, 130
,, "St. Paul" at	114
,, Thanksgiving Service at	114
"St. Peter," Benedict	116, &c.
Stainer, J.	89, 118, 129
Stamp Duty	60, 61
Standard Glee Book	88
Stanford, C.	134
,, "The Revenge"	138
State of Music	8
,, popular taste	27
Statistics of work done	141
Stereotyping	12
Sterling, Antoinette	128
Stirling, Elizabeth	59
Stockhausen, Herr	107
Stone, Dr. W. H.	106
Store Street Rooms	25
Study of the Violin	130
Sullivan, A.	89, 134

	PAGE
Sullivan, A., first composition (note)	89
"Sunlight of Song"	119
Surman, Mr. J.	42, 49
Surrey Chapel Music	34
,, ,, Psalmody	50
,, Gardens	68
Svendsen	112
Tallis and Birde's Patent	6
Taxes on Knowledge	31, 33, 37, 59
Teaching by correspondence	130
Temperance Societies	48
Text Books	33
Thematic Catalogues	62
Theory of Musical Composition	41
Thomas, Goring	134
,, Theodore	128
,, W. H.	110
Titiens, Mdlle.	88
Tomlins, W. L.	128
Tonic Sol-fa translations	87, 120
Tours, Berthold	117, 129
Townshend, Pauline D.	135
Trade Rules of Printers	31
,, Unions	33
Troutbeck, Rev. J.	114, 129
"Trumpet" Overture	104
Turle, J.	114
Undergraduates of Oxford in 1837	20
Vamping	26
Verdi, G.	110
,, "Requiem"	110
,, Visit to England	110
Village Bands	81
"Vintage Song," Loreley	112
Vocal Association	79
,, Music	42
Wagner's Music	110, 132
Walmisley, T. A.	81
,, T. F.	79
Walsh's Plates	62
Webbe, S.	4, 62

	PAGE		PAGE
Weber	32, 40	Winch, W.	128
Weldon's Divine Harmony	6	Winter, P. von	40
Weippert's Quadrilles	25	Worcester Festival, 1881	134
Wesley's Psalter	50	Works on Musical History	63
Wesley, Dr. S. S.	112		
Westbrook, W. J.	112	Yorkshire and Lancashire Choral Societies.	30
Westminster Abbey	9, 86, 130		
Whitney, Myron	128		
Wilhem System	47	Zerrahn, Carl	128
Willis's Rooms	25	Zimmermann, Miss	118

For EU product safety concerns, contact us at Calle de José Abascal, 56–1°, 28003 Madrid, Spain or eugpsr@cambridge.org.

www.ingramcontent.com/pod-product-compliance
Ingram Content Group UK Ltd.
Pitfield, Milton Keynes, MK11 3LW, UK
UKHW041418180426

11947UKWH00007B/190